A Man For Every Purpose

MY NAKED JOURNEY
SEARCHING FOR LOVE

BASED ON A TRUE STORY, MOSTLY . . .

KATIE L LINDLEY

COPYRIGHT

Victoria Street Publishing

ISBN-13: 978-1979210324
ISBN-10: 1979210322

Book cover design by Melinda De Ross.
Book interior design by Author's Assembler.

Happy Reading

This book is dedicated to my parents, Chris and Avonelle. My mother, who either read me a story before bed or made one up. And to my father, who showed me how a man is supposed to love a woman by continuing to love my mother.

Katie Findley

PREFACE

"I am good, but not an angel. I do sin, but I'm not the devil. I am just a small girl in a big world trying to find someone to love."

—MARILYN MONROE

I LAY HERE, NAKED, EXCEPT FOR MY COTTON BATMAN UNDIES, ON top of near perfect sheets.

Another bed, another man.

I offer my love host a pleasant good morning smile, politely including a postcoital closed-mouth kiss. I toddle off to tinkle in yet another bathroom. My host followed me with his eyes as I tucked into the privacy of his bathroom.

When did the search for true love become so random, hopeful, and hopeless all at the same time?

My hair is disarranged, and dark circles raccoon my still sleepy eyes. I am utter imperfection.

I called out a request. "Honey, how about a cup of coffee?"

No matter who the man is, coffee is part of the deal.

Has romance come down to this? The coffee in the morning? Maybe I should buy a really nice coffee maker and give up. Alone for life, with Mr. Folgers, Mr. Starbucks, or Mr. Juan Valdez. That's it! A *hot* Latin kick-start to my morning. I am not sure if I am looking for romance in the right places, but coffee seems to be a common denominator among the men I choose.

There is something intriguing about falling in love so many times. It is not failure, just small snippets of welcoming intimacy. A window into what could have, should have, might have been. I would rather have a heart filled with these windows than not.

I wish I could count the men I've been with on one hand. I wish I could just stop counting altogether. Promiscuity is what some people call it; insanity is what others call it. I call it my search for true love. I have dubbed it "A Man For Every Purpose."

A Man For Every Purpose

"Take your broken heart, make it into art."
—Carrie Fisher

I BELIEVE IN LOVE! SOMETIME IN JUNE OF 2004, A QUOTE LANDED in my email. I printed the quote out and hung it on my refrigerator like a kid's school project. It became my romantic mantra:

"1. Find a man who makes you laugh. 2. Find a man that has a good job and can cook. 3. Find a man that will pamper you and give you gifts. 4. Find a man who is honest. 5. Find a man who is awesome in the bedroom. Most of all, it is very important that these five men need not know one another."

I had no idea at the time that this quote would describe my quest to understand men and myself in relation to men.

> "When you listen to other women's stories, you begin to understand your own better and you begin to find ways back through and with each other."
> —Eve Ensler

Some facts may or may not have been exaggerated for spicy entertainment purposes. Enough detail about certain men may reveal their identities. Denial or admission is up to them. I have not used any names, nor do I wish to "*out*" anyone.

I have been easy on a handful of men because those men will always have a small piece of my heart, shaping me. I do not carry any torches, yet I have affection for them, nonetheless. I mean, it was my journey, but they were in it.

I may have been harder on other men, because, frankly, I have attracted a couple of jerks. Is it a requirement in the course of relationships to date an asshole or two?

All of my men are simply inspired *characters* that dwell in the outskirts of my memories. Love is love. I have been lucky. I have known love.

Men have always been a big mystery to me, starting with the moment I first became obsessed with my Ken doll. Is that what men are supposed to look like? How will I ever meet a man so perfect in my life? I had a gut feeling it was time to Nancy Drew the heck out of this mystery and discover what makes the male species tick. Why do they think, act, and feel the way they do?

I need to know more! I seem to make all the mistakes when it comes to relationships. It is time to do better.

I have studied the male species in one form or another my entire life. I have read a multitude of self-help relationship books that pile up a mile deep. These "helping" books left me with more questions than answers. Do men want bitches? Do they want their moms? Or do men want a reflection of themselves in a skirt? Or is it the girl next door? Please tell me they are not looking for the glossy perfection in magazines, *oh no*, are they? I have been testing my female skills, wide-eyed and waiting for a response, something, anything, to answer the questions looming in my head.

I've remained single for most of my adult life. Single, as in the only available option to check on the form in your doctor's office if you're not married. But I have had my share of men in the form of boyfriends, husbands, fiancés, and yes, even friends. Without knowing, I was gathering a man for every purpose…

Disclaimer: I did not have sex with every man in this story, or even some of the ones beyond the pages that make up my list of a man for every purpose. For that matter, there may be other men I had been naked with that never made it into this book.

If you could handpick multiple men to be in your life, what would your list look like?

Perhaps in some way you have done this already: Gardener, husband, plumber . . . the list can look different to everyone.

I bare all in this book. I am allowing those who read these pages to look right up my skirt and into my none-of-your-business.

I must be terribly courageous or utterly stupid.

Part One

GROWING PAINS

"I miss being a kid. My only responsibilities were running around and laughing a lot. And someone else was in charge of my hair."

—AUTHOR UNKNOWN

G ROWING UP IN ORANGE COUNTY, CALIFORNIA, I WAS IM-mersed in culture from birth. My California heritage dated back to the eighteen-hundreds, consisting of five generations of orange ranchers. A quiet Orange County suburb filled with farmlands and orange groves as far as I could see. Lining the citrus trees were miles of majestic eucalyptus trees that provided a windbreak. The biggest threat was fire season, where fierce hot winds would destroy all in its path.

Rustic Orange County was what I knew, sweetly existing long before it was coined "The OC." Highly recognized from the cookie cutter "reality housewives" that helped kick-start reality T.V., high heels and all.

The chaotic home I was raised in had three loud brothers and a sister that constantly competed for attention. My voice was small and quiet in comparison.

At age six, I remember sitting still on the couch in my childhood home watching cartoons after dinner. My brothers were having their fighting ritual that happened most nights. It felt like they hated each other. I seemed to be able to turn a blind eye and tolerate this aggression. Then one moment I couldn't; a panicky feeling of the unknown ran through me. Stunned, I began breathing too fast. I had no idea what anxiety was or that it could attack me at any given time. For me, these unsettling feelings quickly turned into hiccups.

Fearful of being teased by my siblings, I ran into the hallway while trying to catch my breath. It was bizarre and scary, but I didn't want my siblings to know. I tried to fix it myself. I would plug my nose, hold my breath, or change my breathing pattern—anything to stop the invasion. I was small and alone, drowning in interrupted air.

These uninvited attacks frightened me. I didn't understand what was happening to me and why. I kept my panic attacks a secret, not wanting anyone to know that something was wrong with me. A year after they first began, I believed I was managing fine on my own. My first grade teacher announced to the class that she was "testing us." Those two words brought on the hiccups for the first time.

Oh no!

Alarmed, I desperately raised my hand to leave the classroom. I had to find my breath.

Standing outside the big blue door of the classroom, hiding in the hallway, I tried to trick myself out of the moment. None of my usual solutions were working. I pinched my nose, closed my eyes, and walked backwards in a circle. Somehow, it worked.

No one ever caught me performing these bizarre rituals I used to manage my breathing. These episodes happened to me in every grade all the way through college. The only thing that changed was my size. My private internal dysfunction did not waver. I never became cavalier or glib about it, maybe annoyed, but always frustrated that I was out of control. I never grasped why.

Growing up, I was a skinny, long-limbed, awkward, tomboyish girl with dishwater blonde hair. Daily, my hair would get caught on the back of my chair at school—that small silver bolt had it out for me. My solution was to rip my hair from the trap that bound me to my seat. I left the chair with the fringed look of a bad idea. I didn't care– bad hair I could manage.

I wanted to climb fences and ride horses, and pretty hair was not required for that. The freedom that I knew while riding through orange fields brought me a sense of power, control, and calm. Never once did I hiccup while on the back of a horse. I was filled with peace. I was in charge.

Being Full Grown Doesn't Equal Being Grown-Up

"It's the Peter Pan in me, I don't think I'll ever grow up."

—Jason Behr

Throughout the years, I discovered the warrior in me. The anxiety attacks of my youth had to take a back seat. I had to connect with the powerful girl I once knew on the back of a horse.

Being a single mother of three, I was not going to let my history or age factor into my quest for finding true love. I stood in the face of all ill-conceived or pre-conceived notions and did my best to prove them wrong. There are single men and women of all ages everywhere. What is up with a society that is so crazed on youth? We have to be young to be marriage material?

Marching forward onto my journey into the darkest of nights, I waited for the dawn. Bucking up against the odds. I'm not so sure that the odds were against me. I am one person, not another statistic.

Now I'm all grown-up, or at least *way* taller. I've never subscribed to well-known sayings such as, "A woman over a certain age (40) has a better chance at getting struck by lightning than finding a husband."

Or was it being hit by a bus? Why such a horrible fate for the aging female? No other viable options other than singlehood, an act of God, or an ill-timed bus? Why is *she*, any woman over a certain age, too old or no longer a desirable option on the marriage-market? Is *he* lost? Is "*he*/future husband" elusive, uncatchable, a rare species? Never to be found by the girl who has seen her prime and is in rapid decline toward a mediocre celibate life with cats? No . . . no damn way!

Bare-footed and standing in the kitchen on the cool slate floor, I reflected back to the mantra I had hanging on my fridge. How hard can it be to find a man (or many men) for different purposes? I can do that!

I proceeded to gather my team of guys. My intentions were light-hearted. I thought, "Why not?" I didn't have a serious commitment at the time.

So, that was the point in my life when I decided to set forth on my exploration, titled: A Man for Every Purpose. This endeavor would consist of a few variables. I was to market myself in my little corner of the world as the saucy OC woman I had always been. The only change I was making in my life would prove to be my attitude about love.

Before this "Ah-ha!" moment, I had hidden my spirit and soul from those around me—guarded to a certain extent for my own protection. From this juncture forward, I proceeded to make myself available, both physically and emotionally. This was my time to shine and leave the hiccupping days behind.

It wasn't about approval. I was on a mission. An expedition, a quest, a man-hunt, to understand men.

Oh no! What does a woman wear when she is on a man-hunt?

Ah ha, that's right, a dress.

I love men, but they continued to bewilder me. What did I have to lose? I would, at the very least, learn about these hairy, testosterone-filled creatures. Or maybe, better yet, and more importantly, learn about myself in direct relation to the opposite sex. At that time, it was easier to look at them than it was to look into the mirror, but it took me a long while to understand that.

I set forth on my journey to make friends with a number of men. Was my list the same as the one on the fridge? It kind of was, but it wasn't until I had a baseball team of guys that I discovered this truth. I ended up with a list that looked like this: I found a man to help me with my car. I found a man to help me with computers. Another man took me to numerous lavish parties. I also found a man that could take me on wild Harley rides. Oh, and there was another man with a not-so-specific purpose. His role always seemed to confuse me. Maybe his sole purpose was sex? *Okay*, my list was not as perfect as the quote hanging on my fridge, but I did my best.

Love is a poetic contradiction. It is also the greatest risk, as it exposes all of one's being. It is uncertain. It is vulnerability at its finest. It can painful. It is strong. It is caring. It is forgiving. It can shake you to the core and demand you to retreat to that all-too-familiar position, curled up on the floor. Or it can send you soaring high into the clouds, floating on hope and happiness.

I would like love to just be still. I would like to be still with love.

Love —it is a choice; it is a truth. Being helpless and somehow feeling unworthy of one's soul given right to love is saddening, vacant, and cowardice. I will leap towards love with a full heart; life without love is not for me.

I understand that it's possible my hand may be forever attached to a leash with a beautiful tail-wagging dog on the other end. Or that I might fall in love with my sexy, saucy, single self. My kids are grown and it is time to unravel this mystery and forge ahead. I deserve love; we all do. I am ready for it and definitely expecting it. When love shows up, so will I.

I hope.

First Comes Love,
Then Comes Marriage, Then...

"Love doesn't make the world go 'round. Love is
what makes the ride worthwhile."
—Franklin P. Jones

Before the idea of A Man For Every Purpose came along
in life, I was a one-man kinda' gal. I thought my love story began
and ended with the first man I ever really loved, the first man I ever
married.

Had that been the case, this book wouldn't be in your hands right
now. And what great book begins and ends the same way?

I met Dream Mate when I was twenty. The age of a girl who be-
lieves she's learned all she can learn about life, men, and the world
around her and is ready to take it all on, shoulders back, no fear. I was
that girl, dancing to the theme song of innocent ignorance.

Dream Mate was the handsome, East Coast, sporty/preppy, love
story kind of a guy who appeared on the scene in my small town of
Dana Point, California. He stood six feet tall, with thick hair that was
almost unmanageable, and the sharp chiseled features of a GQ model.
His looks reminded me of a blonde Ted Danson when he starred in the

TV sitcom "Cheers." Dream Mate's blue eyes were set just a bit too narrow—and rarely landed directly on the person who held a conversation with him. They were the epitome of mystery.

I was quick to disregard him. He was the hot bartender that rode into town; it was best not to stand in that line. That line of his had fresh and saucy girls numbered deep. I would rather watch that show than be a part of it.

Every girl wanted him, but I was the only one who rejected him, smiling, rolling my eyes and walking away. It seems obvious now, of course, but there is something to be said about how I behaved because he had to have me.

I was spoken for at the time, living with my high school boyfriend, who had helped me escape my childhood home. Not that I was being held hostage. My folks were by and large ideal and deeply loved one another. But I was curiously expectant and longed for what adulthood and self-reliance would feel like.

With reluctance, after Dream Mate heavily pursued me, I agreed to go on one date. My current boyfriend was gone more than he was present, and his fidelity was highly questionable. Curiosity got the best of me, and I decided to investigate this East Coast charmer without feeling a drop of guilt. I had all the hope and freedom of a girl of twenty.

Our date took place in the late morning. I skipped up to him with an open heart and playfully jumped into his arms, wrapping my long, gangly legs around him.

Did I find a home there in his arms during that first date?

We headed north to Laguna Beach to spend our day walking about the sandy beaches and tide pools. Laguna Beach is a quaint Southern California beach town winding around the coast. The architecture is that of a European village, with downtown shopping and hills abundant of million-dollar cottages that capture a view of the Pacific Ocean.

We shared a long, picturesque summer afternoon in balmy, warm wind that kissed our skin as we went about our first date. It was the kind of perfection you often see on postcards. Surrounded by sunlight and warmth, we experienced an eternal feeling of now dappled with youthful hearts. Nothing could be wrong in our world, as we were coming together with every ounce of magic that happens when you are falling in love.

We went to the rocks that sit above the surf and talked about our lives, childhoods, and dreams. The air was salty as we sipped on our banana-date smoothies. Dream Mate was attentive, and, for that day, he never took his blue eyes off of me. I felt so girlish and was clearly falling for the boy I had been pushing away.

Ending the evening at an expensive, funky, Laguna Beach restaurant, he looked at me and couldn't eat—he was lovesick. It had been the perfect day; I didn't want it to end. Being near him, spending time with him, I was happy. I was home.

Dream Mate was unable to finish his meal. He threw his white napkin on the floor as a symbol of surrendering to our powerful connection.

After dinner, while sitting in Dream Mate's car, I glanced at him and saw a clear vision of him as an old man. In that instant, with great certainty, I realized I would know him for the rest of my life.

I wasn't sure how I felt about that. My first thought was *no*.

But fate, and my heart, had something else in store. As a result of that enchanting date, we became inseparable. I packed up and moved out of now ex-high school boyfriend's house within the week. It was desperately fast, but my heart had a sweet hope in it. I simply followed that hope into my future.

I never stopped to question if my dreams were coming true; every day was a dream that rolled into the next salty-air-filled day.

I found sleep like I had never known. Dream Mate was my peace. My heart rate slowed and my safe place was near him. Lost was any sign of panicked breathing, as hiccup-girl faded peacefully into my past. I found my heartbeat; I found my breath. I was at rest with myself. I slept better with him than without him. This precious feeling would hold true inside my soul for this one man. How was I to know the depth of the effect it had on me at age twenty?

Dream Mate once told me that the first time he saw me, he knew we would be married. As it turned out, he was right.

Lying in the back of his Toyota pickup truck, camping with our two dogs, the fall leaves surrounded us. The sun came up, casting dappled shadows. We were engulfed by trees and leaves holding us in our safe bubble. It was quiet. The covered cab we were nestled in had the stale odor of dogs and crisp fall hanging in the air.

Dream Mate turned my face towards his and looked me in the eye.

"Marry me, just say *yes yes yes yes yes*," he said.

It was romance kicked up. I never answered, I never had to. There was no real question there.

Looking into his meaningful eyes, I just said, "I need to go to the bathroom." We continued on our great camping adventure and started to plan our wedding; it was that simple.

I was twenty-two and Dream Mate was twenty-five when we were married. We became pregnant six weeks into marriage. Our first bundle of joy arrived, and we were parents! Life was fun; I married my best friend. We played well together, and day after day was so very heavenly. Days easily turned into months and years as our family grew seamlessly.

Then, perfectly planned, three years later came our second bundle of joy. Just like our first, we had a blonde-haired, green-eyed baby to match.

Did I mention the two yellow Labradors, the white Volvo station wagon, the yellow 1973 Mustang convertible, and a home near the beach? Nauseating, right? We were the whitest, shiniest couple within miles of the whitest county of Orange. It was uncomfortably pristine. White on white on white.

Dream Mate and I were so picture-perfect, we could have modeled for Ralph Lauren, *gag*.

One full day folded into the next, living the dream, or so I thought. Then again, what was I thinking? I married the hot bartender.

Seven years into our togetherness, something was terribly wrong, and I had no idea what. The wife really is the last to know. I had an ulcer. I was too young to have that type of stress-related affliction, but I had it nonetheless.

My uncle was an old-fashioned family doctor. I went to see him to help with my current illness.

"How's your marriage?" he asked me.

I must have hesitated, because my answer with a smile on cue was delayed. My uncle knew before I did. I didn't have time to even consider the unthinkable. I was busy with our home, dogs, and two babies. My hands were full.

Did I neglect us? Did I forget to love him? Did I stop paying attention to him? I didn't think so at the time. I thought I was loving him by taking care of our babies.

Dream Mate was spending less time at home, and when he left with our two young children, they would often have chance meetings with the "new gal" from his office.

I was still in dark denial. This could not be happening. He adored me, and I adored him. Was I really so lost I could not see what was right in front of me?

There was no way I had the ability to confront the horror that was eating at my gut. As the saying holds true, we do the best we can with what we know at the time. I was holding onto a lie; it was safe.

Then the credit card bill came. Dream Mate had been shopping in the women's department at Nordstrom. I saw the bill and called the store to inquire about the purchase, which turned out to be a black leather jacket. They even told me the size: 2. I was size 4. Nordstrom knew before I did. Still, that was not enough for me. We signed up for the 'forever package,' we loved each other, damn it!

One night, after tucking the kids into bed, I heard Dream Mate on the phone in the kitchen using a soft voice. Every hair stood up on my body as I crept downstairs where I could better listen to him. I sat with my back against the wall; he was less than ten feet from me. I felt sickness rising from my stomach. He offered to help the person on the phone move. He was being so thoughtful and sweet.

I recognized that voice. I remembered that voice. I fell in love with that voice. I was reeling. That voice was now someone else's? I waited, sitting against the wall, until he hung up. As he walked from the kitchen, the sight of me startled him.

I confronted him then, allowing the horror in me to rise up and come out. Pleading from a place inside of me I did not recognize.

"Who were you talking to?" my unfamiliar voice cracked.

"Just tell me . . ." I pleaded.

He went into full deception mode and offered me nothing but to go back to the state of denial.

"No one, just a friend," Dream Mate said.

Leaving me to continue to embrace dishonesty. I was shaking and crying. I knew better, but I knew nothing.

Say It Ain't So!

"I've been heartbroken. I've broken hearts. That's part of life, and it's part of figuring out who you are so you can find the right partner."

—Heidi Klum

Days went by, as days do. Sleeping next to him, but feeling a divide. It was strange but real. Our sex remained consistent. However, I knew on some unwanted but deep level that the sweet innocence of our lovemaking had changed.

One afternoon, we were together like we had been countless times. Afterward, he rose from our bed, and, speaking to himself, his words spilled from his lips in a quiet voice.

"I can't do this anymore."

I never responded. I did not need to. I knew him. I knew what he meant.

It took weeks and days, moments, and many months, family dinners and making love, Dream Mate mowing our lawn and playing with our kids, before he finally left. He never really moved out. It was a sneaky, covert operation, one gym bag at a time. Dream Mate seemed to always be on the sly, and him departing was no different than having him "there." We never had an honest conversation about the collapse of our marriage, very few words, just a painful absence. For far too long he went back and forth between us both.

I found out later from a girlfriend I did step class aerobics with that this New Gal of Dream Mate's was voted in college by her sorority sisters "the most likely to marry a married man." Well, good for her—she deserved that trophy. Too bad her victory played its part, just a part, but a part nonetheless, in what disassembled a family, my family, our family.

It felt like New Gal stole my identity, as Dream Mate and New Gal would take off on the same adventures that I shared with Dream Mate and our children. It was utterly strange to me, watching a different woman sit in the passenger seat. That woman was no longer me.

It was not her fault. I don't blame her. She did not have that much power. Dream Mate and I married; Dream Mate and I messed up our marriage.

My life slowly started to shape up like a big, fat cliché. At age thirty, ten years after we came together, we were separating. He changed dance partners. Do-si-do.

I became very bitter toward him. Scorned does not look pretty on anyone; Botox cannot fix that look. Holding anger toward another person is like drinking poison and wanting them to die; wasn't that a Buddhist saying? I made myself sick with aching disappointment and contempt. I was not even close to looking at myself. I had an unhealthy victim attitude that this was all happening *to* me and *to* our children.

On one occasion, our children were visiting Dream Mate and his New Gal. The kids phoned me. As I was chatting with the little ones, Dream Mate and New Gal chimed in. I could hear their painful comments in the background.

"Too bad she doesn't have a life."

They were laughing at me, and I could hear them. It was harsh and true. I didn't know my life; I didn't know myself. I never saw myself as a young divorcée with two small children. As Dream Mate and his New Gal made fun of me with their cruel comments, I became even more sour, shrouded in self-hate. This felt so awful. I wish I had some of the grace that took me decades to find. I was empty.

I look back on this time as devastating. I was shattered, broken, and my choices reflected exactly that. At thirty years young, I did not have enough life experience to handle what I was going through. The life I had been living was ending, and I wasn't ready for it.

My future plans with Dream Mate included a recommitment ceremony every ten years—a love for a lifetime. How could I have gotten my entire life picture so utterly and completely wrong?

Out Of Denial Into Divorce

"Divorce is never a pleasant experience. You look upon it as a failure. But I learned to be a different person once we broke up. Sometimes you learn more from failure than you do from success."

—Michael Crawford

Dream Mate was my best friend, or so I thought. I needed to seriously question myself, but sadly I didn't.

Instead I turned to hot baths. Sounds crazy, but with children ages three and six, the bathroom was the only place I could ease my pain. I found solace in the awaiting bubbles. I poured my broken heart and aching body into the tiled refuge. I began to soak three or four times a day.

Why is it that women find sanctuary in the bathroom? Architects should absolutely take this into consideration.

I could not reason myself out of what was happening in my life, nor could I turn off the pain. I begged for the future to show up, because I could not handle those dark days. I had two beautiful children and a bitter attitude. I did not match my growing children. It was not a pretty site. I was consumed with playing the victim and my hands were bleeding from wanting to hold onto a future that was no longer mine. Bewilderment guided me as I tried to fake it from day to day.

I couldn't eat, and I began to dwindle away. At five foot ten, I have always been on the thin side, but my reflection looked much like that of an ill patient. I was standing in the shell of a girl I didn't know.

The one person I could always turn to was gone; he had vanished into the arms of his secretary. I was living out the movie of the week. I was truly in a place that begged for insight into the future. My soul seemed torn apart and I was stuck inside a vortex of crushing pain.

I was alone.

On the surface, I stood tall, and embraced our children with a smile. As parents, we put on a brave front, but kids are much more intuitive and pick up on all those things you think you are being clever about hiding.

One late afternoon, while Dream Mate was standing at the doorway ready to exit, our three-year-old stood on a spot in the middle of the staircase and observed.

She glanced up at me.

"Mommy, can we get a daddy that isn't going to leave?"

I stood in silence as I looked at Dream Mate and at our daughter.

It was awful.

Who are we kidding?

They know.

At the time, I was prideful in thinking I *could* find a new daddy for my children. I was terribly wrong. I hate myself for thinking a person is replaceable, or a relationship for that matter. How could I find a great daddy/husband when I didn't even understand where *my* fault lay in this mess? I blamed it on being young. I was an idiot and I was lost.

When one is in the throes of divorce, life as you know it seems unrecognizable. You utterly lose your sense of normalcy. What feels like a death turns out to be a divorce.

When there is a death, you wear black and people bring you casseroles, mostly lasagna—let them know if you are gluten free. When there is a divorce, people are awkward and don't know what to say, especially if you're standing beside two beautiful, young children. Standing in front of failure is uncomfortable.

The sad stares never utter, "Oh I saw this coming, he was quite the *rover*," but you hear it all the same anyway.

I avoided any conversation with simple acquaintances. I became far too good at being anonymous. I was constantly blending in without establishing any real connection with others, slipping in and out of places. Are broken homes where broken people lived? I dare not look at that question. I had to survive. *We* had to survive.

I was a smiling shadow.

I started searching desperately for a new normal. What did that look like? I had no idea. I was lost in a sea of grief and was being tossed about by my own sorrow. When you lose something and search for something else, it can become quite a destructive process. It was way too easy. I began to self-destruct.

Dream Mate made a half-fickle attempt at returning to our marriage weeks before his wedding to New Gal. I allowed him into our bed. That was easy. Letting him come back, that was impossible. Confused and bitter, I simply shut down my heart.

Dream Mate moved on and got married. It was sealed; there was a new Mrs. Dream Mate.

This pushed me further into utterly losing my sense of self. Someone else filled my shoes. It was bizarre.

If she was now Mrs. Dream Mate, who was *I*?

I was a firm believer in supporting marriage. Sounding frightfully sanctimonious, I supported their union. I may have gone overboard in this display of support, insisting that our children be present at their wedding. His new bride did not approve, stating,

"This is *my* day!"

I even bought them a wedding gift. Uh, never got a thank you note, *rude*. The moment my children loaded into their uncle's car for their dad's wedding, until they were returned, I cried. I sobbed all day. I couldn't stop crying. I may have had some unfinished healing?

With Dream Mate being the father of my children, backing his new union seemed to be the best choice. It was awkward, as I was constantly trying too hard to do the right thing. I decided to walk the high road and not look down. That high road is a walk for lonely daredevils, they say, and a long damn drop to the bottom. I think I just got vertigo.

Instead of eating, praying, and loving, I was absent of appetite, bathing and throwing my emotional ailing self onto the *wrong* guy. Basically, I took a wreck and placed it in front of an oncoming train.

This was not good, positive, or healthy. I did not take the time to see my fault in the breakup of my marriage to Dream Mate.

I carelessly skipped over that vital part of healing.

Part Two

WRONG GUY

"I did the best I could, and in some arenas, my best was not good enough. I've made some bad choices."

—AMY GRANT

A S FOR THE NEXT RELATIONSHIP, THE RECOLLECTION OF IT makes me feel sorry for myself, and that is sad.

It all started when I was on a girls' ski trip to Mammoth Mountain. All of the ladies I was with were married. I was freshly divorced, desperately gloomy, pushing thirty-one, and in a sorry state.

On this glorious weekend, where girls just want to have fun, I hit the slopes and dressed like a cute ski bunny, or so I tried.

The Los Angeles Fire Department was having its annual ski week. Yippee! Firemen everywhere! The group of us gals were almost giddy about going out to happy hour to grab a bite to eat. The mountain was filled with hundreds of firefighters; the odds were on our side.

Wrong Guy was a Los Angeles firefighter. He had all the attributes that one would imagine in a fireman. He toted a mustache, his smile was just a bit too big, and he was fit and athletic. He made his way over to me and did the usual pick up at a bar. He bought me a drink and bragged about how fabulous he was. Telling me how much he loved kids, of course. He was also an uncle. They are all uncles, aren't they? Is this stuff just standard when it comes to dating? I had no clue. I was crisp out of a marriage and wounded.

31

Leaving the restaurant, walking through the icy parking lot, I spotted Wrong Guy making out with my married girlfriend.

I mumbled to myself, "Well, so much for him."

I found his buddy way more attractive; he didn't have a mustache. When I saw Wrong Guy with my friend, I didn't care. Turned out, his friend that I found more desirable was not an option, as he was living with his girlfriend.

Again mumbling, "Oh well."

A week after our girls' trip, I was taken aback when Wrong Guy called me. He was charming and filled me with much needed flirtation. Visions of him lip locked with my friend became neatly tucked away. Male attention, wow, that was kind of nice. He asked me to go out on a date.

I am not sure why I accepted his invitation. Seeking male approval after being dumped is easy to see now. The sad place inside of me had words I didn't want to hear, nagging at me to prove Dream Mate wrong; I was *desirable*! Even if I was desired by a man attracted to vulnerable and unavailable women.

Then again, I thought, what the hell, I'll get out of the house.

I met him in Huntington Beach because that was closer to my home than to his Los Angeles home. Getting a babysitter and driving to meet my date was a first on all fronts. I wasn't sure how I felt about it. But, I was clearly lonely.

Like the last two people left stranded on the deserted island of singles, Wrong Guy and I started to date. I was desperately trying to sort out my life. I clung onto this man like he was an answer. He was in no way an answer. I was part of the walking clueless.

The abuse showed up with subtlety. He would put me down and disregard me. Telling me cleverly worded comments about how stupid and incapable I was. The emotional abuse showed up in a cagey disguise. I sucked it up and allowed myself to be objectified. I was so desperate to have some form of validation that I chose poorly for myself. Maybe 'this-girl-just-got-dumped' was stamped on my forehead, because I was treated as if that was what I deserved.

I read somewhere that we only accept the love we *think* we are worthy of. I learned that, when my self-esteem was utterly shattered, being poorly treated was sickeningly acceptable. I felt deserving of bad treatment. Wrong Guy dished it out to me with ease. I had gone from being overly confident to being okay with a constant barrage of belittlement. He monopolized me, and I never wanted to share with friends what was going on. I became isolated, I became his. That was the best I could do, or so I thought.

Most of his comments, if they weren't cutting me down, had a "sexually dirty" undertone. With Wrong Guy, I became a sexual doll on his assembly line. He would comment on how I looked: my weight, my body, my everything. He even told me how to brush my teeth and wipe my ass, all according to him.

I slipped into a controlling relationship without knowing it. On the surface, it seemed like other relationships—going out to dinner and social events. Behind the scenes, or under his breath, were comments that consistently tore me down.

I had an epiphany about Wrong Guy on a Saturday night. He decided to stop by his mother's house to check up on her, and she hid in the closet until he left. Wrong Guy fixed her running toilet and was at her home for nearly twenty minutes.

If Mom hid from her own son, what am I missing? This was obviously a red flag.

Wrong Guy was dangerous and convoluted. I was not going to allow this man to control me any longer. The little things added up, added up to the end. I lacked the ability to see things for myself. It was through the story of his mother that Wrong Guy shared with me that I started to pay closer attention. I did not yet have the capability to find my own way. I had to follow clues from others.

The Christmas before I broke off the relationship, Wrong Guy drove one hour to my house, quietly crept in unannounced, and stood at the foot of my bed with red poinsettias in each hand. He loomed over me in the dark, hovering over my sleeping body. Wrong Guy looked like a shadow from the depths of my nightmares. Terrified, I bolted upright, sitting, staring at this image in disbelief. No words could come to me; it felt like I had been in an accident. I thought it was the beginning of the worst horror movie, all taking place in my own bedroom. My heart pounded loudly, and finally I found my words,

"What are you doing?" I was grateful I sounded strong.

"I just wanted to bring you poinsettias," he answered.

"Now, at midnight!? You scared the crap out of me. I was asleep."

"I'm sorry."

Wrong Guy sounded wounded and sad. He was hurting, and that posed its own element of threat.

I gathered myself together enough to walk him to the front door and let him out. I tried to remain calm, but that night sleep would not return to me.

Who would sneak up on a person like that? This man was unstable and unsafe for me. Did Wrong Guy think he would find my bed with another man in it? I'll never know.

Wrong Guy had deep pockets. However, no amount of money was going to change my mind. I was at the point of no return. I was gaining strength, I had more than myself to worry about. I had two children, and I would never put them in harm's way. My children and I needed to get away from this man.

After that near miss, I took a little time off from dating. As it turned out . . . *far* too little time off.

NUMERAL DUCE

"Don't you know there ain't no devil, it's just God when he's drunk."

—TOM WAITS

FASTER THAN YOU CAN SAY, "ARE THERE ANY MEN LEFT?" ECHOING into the abyss, the lingering question follows, where did all the missing men go?

I met husband Numeral Duce. He was younger than me by five years. I was thirty-three, almost thirty-four. Numeral Duce had all the answers. Whether he had knowledge on a subject or not, he either knew or made up an answer for it (and he was right, dammit!). He was the definition of a know-it-all. That should have flagged a warning, but in my desire to get life right this time, I ignored all the signs. I did love how punctual he was. Finally, a man I could count on!

Right?

Numeral Duce had little to no forehead. Anything reminiscent of a forehead was engulfed by his curly hair, wired too close to his head, reminding me of a Chia Pet. His beautiful high cheekbones set off his face in a flattering manner, yet he always seemed a little awkward with himself. His grey/green eyes darted about, and when they first landed on me, he gave me a double-eyed squint. I think this was his flirty face. I liked that squint. It signaled to me that he was pleased with me in that moment. He was tall, standing close to six foot four; his long legs would stride out, walking two steps for my every one, and he never looked back to see if I was left behind. We did not take time to get to know one another.

As much as opposites can attract, we did. Our relationship was a cosmic insult to the universe.

Numeral Duce attended the same church I did. Before I could blink, we were married, blending three children, and going for a fourth. This unraveled as quickly as it began. It seemed as if we were far too opposite to be together. I never had a best friend in him, and I was learning the hard way that I may never find what I had with Dream Mate again. The same deep soulful connection was never present with Numeral Duce. Why would it be?

It was a huge mistake to try and hold up my first marriage in comparison. This was completely unfair to myself as well as to Numeral Duce.

We went to three different counselors. All three told us we would end up divorced. Even the soft-spoken pastor held no hope for us. We were doomed. I was stubborn and cavalier, and these prideful qualities never served me. I had my hand in this failed attempt at a family.

He was a drinker of beer, *too* many beers, every single night. He would oftentimes get nasty with his words, mostly the words that were directed at me.

I felt like a doormat. Fetching his beers, he mocked my subservience in a cruel way. After all, this is what our fabric was, the image of the perfect churchgoing family. I fell under the umbrella of being the dutiful wife. I handled this behavior for the sake of the "family picture" I was desperately trying to fulfill. The very picture I seemed to have messed up with my first marriage. I had to do better! I felt the tug of having one more baby; my biological clock was ticking louder than the Big Ben in London. I was thirty-four, almost thirty-five. I felt the now or never.

What was I willing to go through to get it right? On the surface, everything looked good.

On one typical Friday night at our home, my oldest son, who was eleven, was sitting next to his stepdad on a green custom-made couch. Numeral Duce attempted humor directed at me, but it was awful and mean in spirit. His sarcastic words shot at me and I did not duck.

My son looked at his stepdad and then at me. His glancing eyes seemed to connect that this was how men were supposed to behave towards the women they loved, the women they married. That moment terrified me. *No way* on God's green earth would I allow my son to grow up thinking this was the way to treat a woman. Any woman. Hell no!

Sadly, my conviction laid with doing right by my children. I was a walking contradiction. I wanted to instill certain standards upon my children that I couldn't instill within myself or my relationship choices. My self-worth did not hold the same value as the worth of my children.

I was formulating plans to leave our marriage even though I was pregnant with my third child from this mean-mouthed man.

Numeral Duce spent most nights sleeping on the same couch that he drank on. His level of subjugation toward me tipped the scale. I felt torn only because I was knocked up. I had to survive and make the best choices for my children and myself, even our unborn child. My children coming first. These degrading words would never be acceptable to me.

In the beginning, I saw what I wanted to and ignored the obvious signs. Once again, I was the foolish one. It was too late; I would never have my babies grow up thinking this verbal barrage disguised as humor was acceptable behavior. My eight-year-old daughter and I spent far too many nights hiding upstairs, holed up in the master bedroom, out of earshot from his words.

Too much booze can be bad, and, in this case, it was. I was thirty-five and pregnant when he moved out. It was equally my fault as it was his; I allowed him in. Memories of my poor choices were left scattered throughout every room of my home.

NO MEN, NO DATING, NO WAY

"I've been a single parent for a long time. It reminds me of being a waitress. As you walk back to the kitchen, requests come at you from all sides. You're doing the job of two—you have to be highly organized."

—CHERIE LUNGHI

TWO WEEKS AFTER MY THIRTY-SIXTH BIRTHDAY, I GAVE BIRTH TO our son alone, with the company of my doctor and a steady nurse. This is the point in my life where I took more than eight years away from men and dating. With a newborn, a twelve-year-old son, and a nine-year-old daughter, it was the wisest choice.

My wardrobe had gone into survival mode. In a feeble attempt to reject gazes from the opposite sex, I was covering every inch of my body, with buttons done up to my collarbone. My mommy uniform had zero sex appeal. I was outfitted for Battle of the Babies.

I became Super Hero Mommy in those eight years and beyond. Equipped with sensible shoes, a cape, a European station wagon, perhaps even ethereal wings (don't most mothers have those?), I was proactive and involved in bringing up my children. Not a day went by that I wasn't juggling life. School schedules, homework, carpool, after-school sports, projects, yes, the plates were-a-spinnin'.

My home was set up and focused on raising children. I had this notion that I could reflect a "traditional family picture" and made every effort to do all of the traditional things. Like birthday parties, sleepovers, and all the major holidays, I did my best to create memories. My kids often had friends spend the night. Our budget was, more times than not, pancakes for dinner. My daughter's Jewish girlfriend loved it so much because she could splurge on apple-smoked bacon like there was no tomorrow.

My favorite days were "Jammie Days" where we would all stay in our pajamas all day. Reading, building a fire in the fireplace, watching movies, and cooking. On one of our Jammie Days, my youngest son and I went out on a much-needed errand where he announced it was "Jammie Day" trotting around in his pajamas. He got free gelato, as his level of cuteness was through the roof.

I put my emotions aside and turned my eyes away from looking at all the married couples and families around us. If I looked close enough, I would feel sorry for myself and my choices. I did not have time for that. My job was clear, I had three young people I had to usher off to adulthood.

I was taking life one full day at a time. My days were lost in a list of chores, and none of those details included taking care of myself. Raising children is exhausting, I won't lie. And an exhausted thirty-six-year-old, buttoned-up woman did not have time or energy for finding Mr. Right. Or even a Mr. Right Now. I set myself aside and was knee-deep in all the details surrounding my brood. A mother can get lost in raising her children, and I did.

Yet, I still found it difficult to deal with my unmet desire to be touched and all that that implies. Behind closed doors, I could get the job done, but it would end there. I longed for human connection. I found myself alone and in tears far too often, and I probably made my kids hug me too much.

There was an obvious lack of balance, but I believed it was the best choice at the time. Especially as Numeral Duce and I had endless legal battles that continued for many years after our divorce.

The war began while I was a mother with a six-week-old bundle in my arms. I found myself standing on the battlefield, also known as the courtroom, before the judge too many times. Fighting for custody over our son, I watched our child get older and older until he was standing by my side, tugging on my hand, looking up at me as I was leaving for court. It became part of our routine. It was time-consuming, costly, and emotionally draining. It brought sadness to all those involved, including but not limited to, Numeral Duce and his family.

Our young man is now in his twenties and has grown up with parents that are very different from one another. Time has healed many wounds. Numeral Duce and I are pleasant towards one another and we are both very proud of the young man that is our son.

COUGAR TOWN

"Did you know when you go, it's the perfect ending?
To the bad day I was just beginning. When you go,
all I know is you're my favorite mistake."

—SHERYL CROW

I FELL OFF THE SEXUAL BANDWAGON ONTO AN OH-SO-OBVIOUS choice. You would think that all those years away from men would have served a greater lesson. I must have had the same mentality I had when I first became single after Dream Mate. My maturity level showed itself in my choices, or lack thereof. I now know that it is not time that heals wounds, but rather, what you do with your time.

Right when a fabulous forties hormone surge kicked in, I found myself attracted to a younger man. Frisky and forty-four, my cub was a blushing twenty-nine.

This was a wrong choice not due to his age, this was a wrong choice because he was my daughter's coach. Every decent parent worth their salt knows that you do not date your child's teacher, scout leader, tennis coach, or best friend's parent. Anything and everything that can embarrass your child should be off-limits.

I was so love deprived that I threw those rules out the window while speeding at ninety miles an hour towards sex. Long-awaited and much-needed sex!

Therein lies that defining moment in life when children view you as a person rather than just a superhero. My daughter is an old soul. She profoundly connects dots whilst bewildering many with her innate wisdom. Throughout her struggles with this new arrangement, I saw the depth of her love for me. She saw me as human. Although she did not accept him, she accepted me.

He was fifteen years my junior and a former professional volleyball player. The truth of the matter was, he was the replica of the statue of David while stark naked. I know that sounds unreal, but it was not. The only difference would be the demure private area that Leonardo gave to David. This Cub had the endowment that David lacked.

I began to understand the misnomer that the size of a man's hand has no relation to the size of *anything* else.

This small-handed man's skills as a lover far surpassed mine, and I was receiving lessons. He had his way with me while we were in the throes of passion. He simply made me come unglued. Cub's touch made its way through my body until I lost every thought in my head.

It was frightening and addictive; I was making up for lost time as fast as I could. The intensity of pleasure I shared with this Cub was out of the world. It also stupefied me into leaving my brain behind.

We had fun for a brief time. I revisited my misspent youth. I was offered a sense of sexual freedom that was new and exciting. We became lost in the moments our bodies shared. I kept a count of orgasms. If we only saw each other three days a week, but I had seven orgasms total, then that would account for the whole week. This was the type of math my mind could calculate. The truth of the matter was this Cub was teaching me things I had yet to discover. My body that had lain dormant was now awakened.

One warm summer evening in Huntington Beach, a quaint beach town, we decided to bike to dinner. Being the "boy" that Cub was, his humble earthly possessions consisted of a beat-up truck with bald tires, one bike, a closet full of volleyballs, two surfboards, and a skateboard. I had on a jean skirt that was just shy of disgraceful. And yes, I was on his bike towing him on his skateboard. Cub had one hand fastened to the edge of the backside of my skirt, diddling around with my thong underwear, hooking onto me like I was a trailer hitch. I was well aware of how much fun I was having. Hauling this hunky dude behind me, it was playtime for me.

This new life was a stark comparison to how serious and manner-tempered I'd been in my early twenties and thirties, raising kids.

Was I having a "Mid-Mom Crisis?" Hell if I know. At that time,

I didn't care. Most of the women I knew were dressed in loose fitting clothes and going through premenopausal moments. They were drenched in the doldrums, or was it drenched in the hot flashes?

I was uncharacteristically content with this setup. The Cub offered me no future, stability, or protection. He offered me only physical affection and playful fun. I was deeply in need of the beautiful human touch that I received from him, no matter how misguided.

Cub brought me back to life, and I am glad for that. Naughty as it was, and as badly as I felt about my daughter, I selfishly forged forward and had a brief affair as a cougar. I figured out that weak in the knees didn't have to equal soft in the head.

I found myself growing wary of picking up every check for dinner. That signaled our time was coming to an end. When he wanted me to help him with rent money, it was time to check in with myself and check out of that relationship.

I would prefer to be the girl, not the mommy.

Part Three

Moving Into A Man
For Every Purpose

"Save a boyfriend for a rainy day—and another in case it doesn't rain."

—Mae West

I STOOD IN MY KITCHEN, LOOKING AT THE "EVERY WOMAN NEEDS a Man" printout hanging proudly on my refrigerator by a tattered but useful "God Bless Your Day," magnet. Coming to the end of my affair as a cougar, where there was no "*man*" present, the thought multiple "men" started to sound just right. I was forty-four and re roar. The power of suggestion was enough for me to get a runn

Katie L. Lindley

IT'S TIME TO START DATING

"I suppose it's like a ticking crocodile, isn't it?
Time is chasing after all of us."
—J. M. BARRIE, AUTHOR OF *PETER PAN*

My very best married friends, Don and Dawn, who happened to be having dinner at the same restaurant as Cub and I one night, took one look at me sitting next to this "man-child" (I must have been wiping food from his face. Well, he needed me to). They pulled me aside and promptly informed me they had single male friends of an appropriate age for me.

I thought, "Yippee! Line them up, please."

I knew that I was more than ready to step away from the first relationship I had had in almost a decade. There are men out there of an appropriate age, and I needed to travel in that direction. In my head and heart, I was done playing with the baby Cub. After the conversation with Don and Dawn, it was complete. I ended it before I found myself raising one more child—*him*.

I welcomed Don and Dawn's quest to find me an appropriate male companion. I had known them for years, and they were the only married couple that embraced me as a whole person, rather than a single outcast.

women are treated in a sea of
ious disease sending us
lights would describe
en had been so obvious
med to cowering in ac-
pe and was grateful for
divide and embrace me.
social gatherings. Cou-
shion for anything. No-
les beget couples. I was

group events where I

other woman as we were

of
dy to
ng start.

omer.

ickly replied. This was a

person I had logged numerous working hours spanning over two years.

I should have been appalled. I wasn't.

It was also hard being single at my kids' sporting events. My daughter was in club volleyball. This was like a part-time job that traveled. We were all over Southern California for tournaments, encompassing hundreds of miles. If fifty percent of marriages end in divorce, then these paired off "volleyball parents" were waiting until their kids were grown. *Ugh.*

I was once again the oddball out in the group: a single, divorced, smoking hot, oh wait, no, just a divorced, un-included mom.

However, Don and Dawn included me. This couple, who were joined at the hip, always treated me as an addition. During volleyball tournaments, Don and Dawn would have me join them for lunch or dinner. One time in Las Vegas, Don toted Dawn and I around, with an eye out on each of us. We wandered into a shop with very expensive clothes and trinkets from Italy. Don announced that he would like to be able to buy this one dazzling emerald dress for his wife. Like a knight of the realm that boldly stuck a sword into the ground, he had claimed his intentions toward his beloved.

With mixed feelings, I understood, in that moment, that this type of Prince Man really does exist. However, he and I had not yet met. I had not met the Don to my Dawn.

As timing would have it, there was to be a big fiftieth birthday party for one of their close friends. At this party, there were two lovely, eligible, single men.

Once in awhile, you recognize trouble the very moment you see it. Well, the birthday boy was in the front courtyard greeting the guests as they arrived.

He was trouble.

He was simply dreamy, the bad boy in high school that was still the bad boy in adulthood. His boyish eyes twinkled and he approached me with the confidence of a tiger about to toy with his prey. Me being the little lamb that I was, I quivered at the sight of him. Mr. Charming/ Player came in a tight five-foot-ten package with the most beautiful blue eyes that gave Mel Gibson a run for his money.

Little did I know that underneath the Hawaiian shirt he was wearing was one of the loveliest male bodies I had ever seen. I still, to this day, wish I had immortalized him in a painting, as his body was really too nice not to share with the world. I imagine that is what surfing every day for thirty years will get you. No wonder he posed for Playgirl.

We neatly stood eye to eye.

I was toast; the better-choice-for-me men did not stand a chance. The lovely men that my daughter would have approved of, that would have cherished me, protected me, given to me, the good guys, went unnoticed. You know the white hat, trustworthy, hard-working type? I did not give them a second glance, being completely stupefied (once again) by the bad boy.

Whatcha gonna do?

The Player Or The Bad Boy

"Between two evils, I always pick the one I never tried before."

—Mae West

IN ATTENDANCE AT THE PARTY WERE ABOUT SIXTY PEOPLE. PLAYER'S fiftieth birthday party was filled with friends and family.

I thought, "Perfect, he is six years my senior. This was a way better age difference."

The birthday boy gave a speech. He ended it by thanking his best buddy, the host, with a smack on the lips.

Me being the outgoing, silly girl that I am, and a goner already for this man, I boldly spoke up. As I stepped through the crowd, I used my best *come and get me* voice.

"You need to kiss a girl on your birthday."

Without missing a beat, he bent me backwards into his arms and leaned in for a kiss.

The laughs and cheers broke out; it was a success. It might have been embarrassing had Player said, "No thanks, Dear."

Little did I know then that hardly a day goes by that Player does not kiss a girl.

When was I going to re-route this decision cycle? Give me a bad boy, do I need to chalk him off my list? My poor choices reflected a longing to be a lion tamer. *Foolish*.

Player seemed to prey upon the slightly lonely, mildly insecure female. Pathetically, I fit the profile. I was the little lamb, restlessly waiting for the lion, baa baa, barf.

A couple of days after the party, there was a barbecue at Player's house. It was well-known at this point that I liked him and this was his way of getting us together. I knew in my spirit that he was wrong for me. Every time he called I got knotted up, nervous. I did not even recognize my own voice as I stammered away in some nonsensical babble, embarrassingly resembling a schoolgirl crush.

I should always listen to my gut. It never lies. I could not be myself with him at all, which was unfair to both of us. He never knew me because I could never be me.

Player had this "too cool for school air" about him: kind of cocky or peacock-ish, the hot man on campus. There's a reason the lamb and the lion aren't seen together in the wild, getting along, because they do not. I clearly needed to take a class in becoming a lioness. Maybe if nothing else would come of this relationship, I could at least learn that much.

I felt so awkward with him, and, beyond my nerves never being in control, I felt as confused as the little girl that once hid in the hallway.

Our time together was sporadic yet scheduled. I waited by the phone for any kind of attention from Player.

How dumb and desperate was that?

We went away on a couple of lovely weekends and he invited me to his daughter's graduation party. After the party was over and all the guests left, he led me back to his room. It smelled like a mossy candle. All of his clothes were put away and his bed was made.

Player was exhausted from all the work he did for the party he had just created. He tossed me onto his bed with ease. Kissing quickly transformed to lovemaking, which was familiar for us. Yet the lovemaking also went quickly. He lay on top of me and was snoring within seconds. I never felt special with him.

Moments later, his body jarred itself awake, and he found my eyes open, with me lying under his naked body.

At a head-spinning rate, we were dressed, and he was escorting me to my car to leave. I drove away disappointed that I wasn't more to him, even though we shared many moments where he would gaze into my eyes and whisper the loveliest things.

I believed him.

As my girlfriend Healer told me, "I'm sure he meant it in the moment."

Don't they all?

I felt important. I was his girl. Only, no, I really wasn't.

Wow, was I wrong . . .

As it turned out, Player was an infamous, notorious scoundrel, a wanker at best. Now you can see why he's been anointed with this nickname. Player would deceive women by little white lies—a killer combination with those beautiful blue eyes. He had us rotating on a schedule. He would go out with me on a Thursday, another girl on a Friday. Saturday he would have a quickie with yet another girl, and then, just to keep me around, we would a have Sunday barbecue with the gang.

Poor Don and Dawn would get in fights right in front of me about how I was too innocent for this man. But the truth of the matter was that I chose him. They had a bushel of good men for me to meet. All of which are married now, a side note to myself about how I clearly kept choosing wrong.

During this time in my life, Player was my lover. He was my lesson in a painful class I must never repeat. Player's purpose was not only to allow myself to be naked, but to take the naked truth and learn from the obvious. I didn't want a player. My husband cheated, wasn't that enough?

I wanted a real relationship, not to be on someone's bouncing roster. I deserve more. I struggled with my orgasms, and that should have told me something. Player knew what he was doing in the bedroom, but my childish thoughts of wanting a 'boyfriend' confused my vagina. *Note to self*, listen to your vagina. My heart was a runaway train. I fell hard. I opened the door to release myself in a vulnerable way. I was looking for love in all the wrong places.

I was experiencing a painful one-sided relationship that kept me up at night. I needed to stop making myself so available—waiting in the middle of an open field, or on the shelf, as he went in for the kill. I forgot about my own value.

When did I become so desperate?

I believe every girl at some point needs to go through this type of bad boy. Dangerous, challenging, just out of reach, but at a glance looking oh-so-shiny.

I would rejoice if anyone learned from some of my disastrous choices. But, how often does one truly heed warning? Perhaps, a girl must have the bad boy once—in college— then never to be repeated, like a class that is needed to graduate to honorable, worthy men. In some strange way, I must remember to thank Player for helping me complete my course. Pass, although I got a C-minus, I'm sure.

Time to take my lady business to the doctor and get a health clearance.

I still run into Player now and again, and we still have a spark. I hate that we do, but we do. The chemistry between us could light up a small town and could be felt whenever we were within proximity of one another. Momentary weakness pulses through me as my knees go soft and I cannot string together a reasonable sentence. It seems we always kiss without thought or hesitation, and helplessly so. Powerfully confusing, chemistry can be a lie. A blatant, flat-out pants-are-on-fire lie.

Player treated me like he does all women. His intentions were never to harm me, nor did I ever tell him how it tore me up. He did not deserve to know as he never cared deeply enough for me. I was the dummy. He did manage to bring out the ravenous woman in me.

Or was it the desperate woman in me?

It's a coin toss.

It was time to cross the "Player" off my list.

Sexy Harley Guy

"People are more violently opposed to fur than leather because it's safer to harass rich women than motorcycle gangs."

—Alexei Sayle

SOON, ALONG CAME A SPARK, BEHIND THE SOUND OF AN ENGINE that roared down my street. Harley Guy. If he were on the menu, I would order him up with a side of seconds. Just as every woman should date a player once, perhaps on the list of bad boys should be a man with a motorcycle.

Alas, if you cannot, I'll tell you what it's like. The sexy freedom of the road holds me in and takes me away. All while I have my arms and legs wrapped around a man that controls my safety, my life, trusting him at every turn because I have no choice but to trust. Men may buy a fast car and women may hop aboard a powerful bike; both sound a little like a midlife crisis to me.

Roar, mama, I was on a tear.

Harley was older. He stood toe-to-toe with me, with blond greying hair that waved about in the wind, deep blue eyes, and a body with a strong, medium build. He had lines around his smile and crinkle lines by his eyes. I never asked his age, although I could have guessed late fifties. I was in my forties: baby boomer ages.

Flirting and tension lay between us each time we got together and started the moment I met him. I would call Harley up and he would pick me up on his—yes, you guessed it—Harley. He would show up decked out in jeans, bad-ass boots, a white tee shirt, leather jacket, and a black bandana around his neck. I was dressed in leather as I threw my legs over the back of his bike. The neighborhood PTA moms must have blown a gasket at this guy roaring down the cul-de-sac.

What a rush!

Harley and I had long phone conversations. He was a nice guy that owned a printing business and was once in a rock band as a drummer. Of course he was. Another bad boy? I noticed a pattern emerging. We would ride for hours, winding through the hills of Ortega, and I'd have my hands all over him enjoying the thrill. I never climaxed on the back of the bike but have heard it is entirely possible. I could see why.

Each time our ride ended, as he drove up my driveway, we would each check our cell phones and exit to our other dates for the evening. Not before a lingering, minty kiss, of course, before God and the neighbors as our witness. We were bike buddies, never each other's sole interest, and that was just fine for us.

Whenever I start to like a guy, I picture us "together." I hate that I do that, but I do. I found my thoughts wandering off with Harley, even though our relationship was platonic, minus the kisses.

Am I just wired this way? I am.

Do all women think like that? Mentally setting up a sweet home equipped with a great kitchen, down to the details of the dishes, and a Harley in the garage.

I'm a free spirit having more than one man in my world. Really . . . do I want the happily-ever-after romance?

News flash. I do.

I liked my time with Harley. It was always light and fun with a hint of chemistry and a dash of riding on the wild side.

Thank you, Harley. You revved my engines, bringing my bad biker girl out to play.

THE MIDWESTERN MAN

"Go west, young man."

—HORACE GREELEY

MY GIRLFRIEND SET ME UP ON A BLIND DATE WITH OKLAHOMA. He was visiting from Oklahoma and eagerly willing to meet a tall, homegrown, California girl.

We decided to meet at the Chart House in Newport Beach. I walked in and approached a blue-eyed, tall, dark, handsome man. I think he may have had on one of the nicest pair of cowboy boots I had ever seen.

"OK, I can happily roll with this," I thought.

The Midwestern accent dripped sweetly off his lips. I was feeling a bit weak in the knees. Crap, better sit down and get a hold of yourself, girl.

We settled into a window table that overlooked the bay with a view of huge, expensive boats lolling about in the water.

As I toddled off to the bathroom to gain composure, he asked, "Wine, red or white?"

I replied, "Oh, a nice white please. Let's have fish."

He ordered a hundred-dollar bottle. That would work.

I really liked Oklahoma; he was a horseman, skier, yogi, and traveler. Check, check, and check. I love it when things in common pencil out. He had a deep sense that his spirit was supposed to be in California. We dined for a couple of hours, and time disappeared without effort. I did not want the evening to end, so I offered to show him around Balboa Island. We hopped in my car and took the ferry over to Newport Peninsula, which was very romantic.

Walking around the small touristy gift shops that offer meaningless trinkets, seashells, cute clutter, and a large variety of whatnots, I decided to try on a toe ring. Being the hippie girl I am, and possibly thinking my feet are sexier than they are, I wanted to show off my fresh pedicure. Just when I thought I had it all together—my sexy or not-so-sexy moves down—the ring got stuck on my toe. Panic rose within me. I was nervous that the hiccups were going to take me over.

No! Hiccup girl was not welcome!

I forced a deep yoga breath. I had one leg up on the counter trying my best not to display my underwear, or what delicate amount of lacy fabric I had on representing underwear.

Meanwhile, I looked like a circus character performing a great feat, balancing on my other leg that had a slight heel. I am really awkward in heels and never have gotten the gist of them. Being five foot ten, there is no need to add height. My toe was rapidly swelling. The look on my face revealed my terror followed by dreadful embarrassment. My toe was turning red to match my heated face.

Oklahoma saw my panic, and, with great sympathy, he picked up my foot, bent down to meet it, and put my toe in his mouth. What in the world was happening? And, why weren't we doing this back in his hotel room?

The next moment, Oklahoma eased the ring off into his mouth. Voila!

This man showed heroic talent that left me a bit curious. If I wasn't freaking out about my rapidly swelling toe, I may have actually enjoyed myself. If I did not like this man, I would have been repulsed. Thankfully, laughter abounded and we didn't even have to buy the slobbered-on, violated piece of bondage.

I needed to think less of my feet and stop trying to show off to guys that I liked. That was too close of a call.

Oklahoma and I stayed in touch, but, unfortunately, he went his separate way, back to the middle of the country.

Sadly, it was one year before I saw him the second time.

He shared his travel adventures about his friend's "sailboat." This craft was a mere ninety-seven feet long, and they had sailed all over the world. Equipped with a full crew that included a chef.

How incredible would that be?

Oklahoma told me that they were going to fly over to Europe to boat around France. He promised I had an invitation. Images of myself in an Audrey Hepburn look flashed before my eyes: large black sunglasses, a huge hat, and a fantastic scarf catching the billowing breeze. I was already packing. White bikini, don't forget the white bikini!

That phone call came right after I had started up things with a new guy, a man I subsequently had a six-year relationship with. Oklahoma told me he would have a first-class ticket waiting for me to fly out to Monaco in two days. I looked at my new boyfriend and realized timing was everything.

With mixed feelings, I passed. Ah, had I only taken juggling in school! Choices guided my direction daily. Could I have been Mrs. Oklahoma? I will never know.

Oklahoma and I remained friends. My daughter and her boyfriend had traveled east across the country and stayed at his home. Oklahoma waited up until two in the morning for them.

Another time, my daughter and I drove back from east to west and stayed with him. On that trip, I saw him with new eyes. We were both single and there was a moment, very brief, but it showed up. We were getting ready to go out to dinner. I had on a pretty dress, Oklahoma was dressed up and smelling great. Holding eye contact and leaning over his kitchen counter, moving in for our first romantic kiss, my daughter trotted down his staircase into the kitchen, stopping us in our tracks. Nothing was to come of this.

The next morning, my daughter and I hopped back in the car and continued to drive west.

Oklahoma is a lovely man, and I am certain that, after more than ten years of friendship, we are solid.

SERENDIPITY

"Some of the greatest things, as I understand,
they have come about by serendipity, the greatest
discoveries."

—ALAN ALDA

DAWN AND DON INVITED ME TO JOIN THEM AT THE LOCAL BAR FOR live music and dancing. I went to their home and the three of us ended up on their bed watching Ronald Reagan's funeral before we went out.

Part of why I love Don so much is that he is a passionate man with no fear of showing his emotions, good or bad. As Don recalled what a great man Reagan was, the house phone rang.

"Who the hell would call during Reagan's funeral?" Don stated as he picked up the phone and slammed it down with a clatter.

I looked up to that man. To both of them, for that matter—Don and Dawn were a force to be reckoned with.

Afterward, the three of us headed downtown for music.

Dana Point is a small beach town and the nightlife is fairly mild. We sat at a small table and I spotted a girlfriend from across the room. As I stood up to say hello, a man appeared out of nowhere. He was a beautiful, dreamy man. I looked into his brown eyes as we were introduced. He shook my hand, and I left my hand in his as I turned to say hello to my girlfriend.

I felt a strange recognition that I knew him. A knowing, a feeling, almost like an accident where everything is in slow motion.

I thought to myself, "Where in the hell have you been? Why did it take you this long to show up?"

It all seemed so romantic and magical. The eleventh of June, where the promise of summer hung in the air and the promise of romance was felt between Six and I.

He thought I was a summer fling.

I thought he was the love of my life.

We were both wrong.

This was Six. A beautiful man for a wonderful six years. An unmeasurable time that could be measured, as all things can. The man I turned down Oklahoma's boating adventure for. The man that I thought was the end of my search. He was the end of my search for that time.

"That's it, I'm done!" I wanted to shout to the world.

"I found him, see…"

We danced, chatted, and laughed. Wine was flowing. I had on the perfect white summer skirt that had just the right amount of crochet lace. It was the kick off to summer, and the moon was full. The perfect gathering was blissfully happenstance.

Six and his guy friend, Beebe, were out on the prowl that night. Beebe is Six's great buddy; they had known each other since high school. Six brought me over to the table. We all ended up together, as Six formally introduced me to Beebe. Beebe was single and his looks resembled Billy Joel's. I mean, he could play his double.

Around our fateful table was Six, Beebe, Don, Dawn, and myself. Beebe and Six had known 'The Dons' for years, so that night had a reunion feeling to it. I sat in the middle of Six and Beebe as each of them had a hand on my thigh. I felt like the girl in the Exorcist movie the entire night, flipping my head back and forth between the men that flanked me.

Six and I danced, like a scene from a romantic movie. I felt an instant romantic draw toward Six. A pull, a force. I wanted to know him.

I gave Six my phone number, I watched as he typed it into his new phone. When my phone did not ring the next day, I immediately knew he lost it in the excitement of the evening.

My exact thought was, "You knucklehead."

As it was, I was right. When you know, you know.

I patiently waited, understanding that Six would somehow figure out how to reach me.

Meanwhile, first thing Saturday morning, Six called Beebe, frantic that he lost my number. They tried calling information to reach Don, but his number was private. It eventually occurred to Six that he could look up Don's business under California State Licensing and placed a call on Monday morning.

I felt a bit like Cinderella as I waited for my prince. His scavenger hunt for my number was sweet, and he showed persistent interest in chasing after me. That had to be a good sign.

The moment I laid eyes on Six, I knew that he was going to get me off the attention deficit disorderly dating whirl. I felt the power of firsthand manifestation, as my Mr. Six Years had most of the qualities that my current array of men collectively had.

Six treated me to nice things, was affectionate, pursued me, was attentive, had a Harley (I know, I know), and was larger than life. He referred to himself as the tall, dark, and handsome local. That should have been a red flag, or at the very least, a yellow one. Looking back, the flags were very clear.

We fell so quickly and deeply for one another that many of my men just naturally faded away.

Mr. Six Years

"Accept the things to which fate binds you, and love the people with whom fate brings you together, but do so with all your heart."
—Marcus Aurelius

Six and I collapsed inward, fast, and together. We had passion through the roof and could not keep away from one another. Looking into his brown eyes was like diving into a pool while not knowing how to swim, but diving nonetheless. I was hooked and there was no going back.

It must have been somewhat mutual, because we could not keep our hands off each other. We had sex all of the time and everywhere: in the car, on his staircase, at people's homes in the bathroom. This could get you thrown off the dinner party social circuit, but, oh well. We were crazy for one another.

We would sit on his couch and share one glass of wine, taking a sip and then releasing it to an awaiting kiss, like a baby bird accepting its nourishment. This was wine tasting at its finest. I not only fell in love with him, but with his family as well. I was rapidly embraced as familia. That is the Spanish word for family; I was family.

I was a smitten kitten. I was lost in his dreamy Latin essence. This man made me sink into his affection. Six would hug me and rock me back and forth. He had a way of touching me that encompassed me to the brim. I loved being in Six's arms. Six became the object of my obsession. Not a good or healthy thing. I looked away from his controlling behavior and only saw the delight that was between us.

Six was a family man and our youngest children matched in age. He was passionate about the college football team my family had been following for generations. He had an older daughter and two younger daughters. I had two older children and one younger one. We were blending six kids like the Brady bunch. *Nothing* like the Brady bunch. Our parents were both alive and happily married. He was a driven, successful businessman. It was a match.

Oh, but wait, he had never been married. What was that I just heard? Oh yes, the other shoe dropping. I think it was a steel-toed boot.

Fun, fun, fun, and family was ever-present on our agenda. Always a party, birthday, baptism, quinceañera, anniversaries . . . the social schedule we kept up with was full. Getting dressed up was a must. Often times, a mariachi band and dancing took place at these events. Tequila flowed, as did wonderful wine and food.

His mother, whom I fondly refer to as my favorite "mother-in-law," was very special to me. Mother-in-law wears makeup and jewelry daily, and keeps herself fit. Her husband adores her. When I am greeted by her sweet husband, he goes right in for the lips, like any respectable Latino. I quickly learned to concede, allowing his greeting to be what it was, *smack*, right on the lips.

The connection I felt with this family ran deep. Six is Mexican-American and is firmly engrossed in wonderful, colorful culture.

During the peak of our relationship, Six would often call me hours before an event and ask if I could join him. A fancy limo would arrive at my doorstep. This magic black car brought us to the floor of the Lakers game, a sky box at the Angels baseball game, plays, and concerts. We had fun—food and wine was in abundance. This big-time partying would put us down like well-fed babies in the back of the ridiculously long car, stretched out on the generous seats, falling fast asleep.

I loved all of the events and social activities; it was a dream for me. Even when we just went to his parents' home to watch Mexican soap operas, it was fun. The drama of the cheesy shows was easily understood, even though I did not understand the Spanish language. Somehow, I giggled at the right moments. I loved being with this family! By blending our children, my youngest son was able to experience some of this rich culture. It was all family, all of the time, and I loved being a part of this tightly-knit crew.

From Bad To Worse

"At the end of the day, I have always seen the end of my relationships as a personal failure. There is nothing ever pretty in saying goodbye."
—Elisabetta Canalis

I FOUND MYSELF BECOMING LOST AS SIX'S GIRLFRIEND. I COULD never please him, at least not completely. No matter how hard I tried, I fell short. I would make him a perfect dinner and he'd respond by saying, "This is so great. Next time, you could just add green onions on top."

It was so subtle—the compliment with the criticism. I ran toward this dangling carrot trying to please this man to no end. This went on for years, an unending endeavor that left me understanding that I had to learn to please myself.

Six and I mirrored, or shadowed, each other's subconscious insecurities. We drew out the best and worst in one another. As awful as that sounds, it served a deep purpose, and I was willing to go into the scary darkness to come out enlightened. It was nowhere near that simple and took tons of painstaking hard work, but that was the end result. People we are closest to can bring out the worst in us; I embraced many dark moments with Six as a vital life lesson.

Six had a condo at the Westin in Mammoth. The peace and the

luxury of the place was a sweet deal. I felt like the Queen of the castle roaming the slate floor lobby.

Six and I set out to go skiing during one of our snowy trips. His skills on the mountain far outmatched mine. I liked to ease down the slopes, look great in my outfit, and enjoy the powder white view. Six had a whole other idea of what skiing was to be like. It was a competitive sport for him, and he did not understand my peaceful perspective.

The walk down from the Westin involved many steep steps. On one occasion, Six trotted down in his ski equipment to wait for me. I was struggling with walking in my ski boots, carrying the skis and poles, and a male employee offered to help me down the steps. I readily agreed; after all, I was the Queen.

Six was viewing me with disdain. I could feel it halfway down the steps, his condemning eyes. Holding my breath in fear, I knew his anger was coming. When the nice gentleman handed me my skis and parted, Six proceeded to shake his finger inches from my face.

"This is not what skiing is all about!" condemning me he said, his deep radio voice raised.

People nearby could hear, and I was humiliated.

Shoulders back, I bravely responded, "I am going to ski on my own."

I sulked off like a small, determined child that had been scolded. This man of mine could be as mean as an angry dog. He treated me like I was one of his daughters, needing to teach me a thing or two. All of the enforced rules that he embraced, neatly divided his idea of right from wrong. It was always his way, there was no "me" in that.

I ended up enjoying his sweet condo mostly on my own. I felt bad about myself in his presence, and it was a feeling that increased until I eventually found a way to get out of the relationship.

Let me correct that—until I eventually realized I needed to find a way out.

But believe me, I didn't see it for a long, long time. I did not *want* to see it and kept my blinders securely in place. Stuffing down what would otherwise be wrong for me. Hence all the years of this passionate relationship.

Six was more like a husband to me, even though we had separate homes, than Numeral Duce ever was. The intensity of our shared love and the agony of our split seemed to match, both all-consuming.

Like a frog sitting in warm water, it was difficult to notice when it started to boil. The beauty was still there but the strife was increasing.

The frog was boiling to its own death. I was the frog.

I was sensing a change and needed to survive. I needed a change to survive. When I should have been searching for a way out, I pushed for marriage.

Nearing the end of our relationship, we became engaged. Six had never been married and he was pushing age sixty. We had been together nearly six years. When we met, I was turning forty-five. As years rolled on and I was past my fiftieth birthday, I wanted more than a boyfriend. I was tired of going back and forth between our two homes that were neatly placed in bordering towns.

I let him know I would not wait around forever.

"If you're not going to marry me, someone else will," I said, an ultimatum that I threw down.

With ultimatums, a forced change was required. I was being spurred on from my girlfriend *and* my marked year of fifty. Midlife was here, I better be here with it. He asked me to marry him under the pressure I created. I am not sure he ever really meant it.

When his eldest daughter was reasonably reeling from our engagement, triggering her fear of change, Six quickly (with much more sincerity offered in the proposal) un-engaged us.

I was left with a ring in the palm of my hand, my fist tightly clenched around it. My left hand had only briefly been adorned by this insincere piece of jewelry.

I'm never going to get those six years back.

When we broke apart, I inquired with a qualified attorney if I could sue him for stealing my youth. Is there a statute of limitations on that? Nope, it ran out, I got old. One of us was aging and running out of time, and it may have been me.

Fifty, here I come, freshly single, clearly older, and sadly reeling. If this was midlife, I was not a happy camper.

The truth of the matter was, I would not have traded any of my time with Six. We had unsurpassed moments together and loved rather genuinely.

Our breaking apart was horrific on my soul, as it was, I am sure, for him. Honestly, there was so little left of me when I ended it with Six. I was a mere image of myself. During my healing from the relationship, I found myself meek and cowering.

I put off the agony of the breakup by throwing myself onto Rebound Nice Guy.

This only procrastinated what I needed to experience. But I had been there before—the hot baths—and I was naively determined not to do it again.

I had this! Or so I thought.

I tried to outsmart the agony of loss. I just had to.

A Whole New Dating World

"I read and walked for miles at night along the beach, writing bad blank verse and searching endlessly for someone wonderful who would step out of the darkness and change my life. It never crossed my mind that that person could be me."

—Anna Quindlen

After ending things with Six, I threw myself into online dating. I was fresh into my fifties and felt rather brave. I was a newbie to this Internet dating scene. Online dating seemed big, scary, and rather instant. Gone were the days where I met a new guy at a bar, or church, or a friend's barbecue. Now it is the click of a button, a profile photo, and trying my best not to sound desperate.

My thoughts were, "Why wait and figure my crap out with Six when I can jump into the arms of another? Or jump into the largest dating pool ever?"

Thousands of men were there and waiting at the click of a button. This ought to be fun.

There it was. My homepage. It read: "Single, active, loves horses, yoga, skiing, the beach, great bottles of wine, black and white French movies, nice girl ready for a nice guy."

I had a picture of myself on my friend's yacht in Newport Beach that was not half bad.

It was all a nauseating sales pitch. The same as every other profile out there. I was a small fish in a big pond. I became overly active with checking my status and returning to my magic computer to scroll through the possibilities of men who would never hurt me.

I was sore and damaged. In a state of inner turmoil. I decided to mop up my feelings by finding a guy who could fill in the blank. What was a better way than to market myself online? I boldly dove into the unknown, *the world of online dating.*

I found that dating in the digital age was painfully awkward. I had always been a long-term relationship type gal, and rushing towards all of these first dates was weird.

I wasn't sure; had Prince Charming ever posted his profile online?

I was nervous, terrified, and feeling like an altered and desperate version of myself. A true romantic like myself had never envisioned that the quest for love would consist of addictive, frantic scrolling through digital descriptions and images.

I had a "Little Bird" that was chirping at me through her own insecurities to see what was out there for a woman of "my age." Little Bird was a friend of mine who was not content with her life. She lived in the exclusive gated community of Coto De Caza, right down the street to one of the "Housewives" of Orange County. She may have complained about all of the camera people and crew, but she really loved the proximity to the C-minus celebrity.

During my relationship with Six, we spent a great deal of time with Little Bird and her husband. We did couple things together, like football games, dinner parties, drinking, and going to the racetrack to see their horse race. It was all very fun.

Yet, the moments alone with Little Bird let me know she felt grave disappointment in her marriage. She had lost complete trust in love and men altogether somewhere down the line.

When I was off balance, perhaps, I was more susceptible to her broken advice. She often contemplated the single life and wanted to live vicariously through me. I listened to her, and I let her words creep into me with great influence.

Little Bird was not a person that I should have turned to for advice, yet foolishly I did. I sensed that Little Bird had an ongoing fantasy crush on Six. I learned that advice from jealous female friends is toxic.

Nonetheless, off I went, setting myself up for instant dating on two top dating sites. This process was interesting. I'd scroll through at least eight profiles each minute. I couldn't set apart Todd from Tom or Mike from Matt. Why were we all here on these sites? What had gone wrong in our pasts? Is anyone looking for what I'm looking for?

I had good intuition and I thought my goal, deep in the shadows of my heart, was to get away from all the memories of Six. There was too much pain associated with my latest heartache.

I wanted a fresh, new perspective.

That is exactly what I went searching for online.

Rebound Nice Guy

"I'm kind of a rebound junkie. So, when a relationship goes sour, I look at the sweetness in life elsewhere. So, I date a bit. The best catharsis is to write jokes and tell 4,000 people about it."

—Vir Das

I FOUND A MAN ONLINE ONE HUNDRED AND TWENTY MILES NORTH OF where I lived, and he agreed to meet with me. Rebound was a sweet guy that felt out of my norm. He was safe, a peaceful "now and zen" type.

I began to routinely drive three hours north to spend time with my new fellow. Santa Barbara, the American Riviera, positioned in this world as that of the French Riviera. It had always held a special place for me.

One of my daughter's volleyball coaches once stated he "hated" Santa Barbara.

I looked at him incredulously.

"Why?"

He said because it was so "artsy, earthy, and snooty."

I spoke up louder than I intended, saying, "That's why I love it!"

At this point in life, Santa Barbara held my newest boyfriend and miles of fun for us to enjoy. Rebound was a good guy in every sense of the word.

We walked or hiked the beaches and the hills. We did yoga and hit some new cool restaurants on State Street. My soul found rest in this peaceful man. He was lovely and comforting. We were the best of friends.

Somehow, in my wounded state, Rebound took care of me. He was my medicine. Our sex was so different than with Six. Rebound was patient and had a loving touch. There was never any of that fiery chemistry between us, and I was glad for that, because that was the relationship I had just escaped. No need to grieve Six!

I was frolicking on the beaches of Santa Barbara with Rebound Guy.

We always laughed together, and, coming out of a situation that took me months to break away from, laughter was in order. Our energies and spirits connected, and our soulful union brought me peace.

He was older than me and toted white hair. I was fifty-one and he was ten years my senior. Rebound was handsome, had kind eyes, and a dimpled smile. His white hair was thinning on top and he had a comb-over going on. Comb-overs are never, ever, a good idea, not judging, just noting. Our naked time in the sack was mild-mannered. No fireworks, but I was trying a safer holiday.

However, I took issue with the stark-white pubic hair. This was new for me, and it was difficult to come around to the white jungle. I suggested ever so delicately that he try manscaping. Being the good guy he was, he started a wee bit at a time, working his way from the outside in.

This, I imagine, was a big deal for the macho guy.

Rebound was an Iron-Man athlete and frequented the locker room with other males. As Rebound's razor made its way to his maleness, he stopped short. What remained was nothing less than a frosty white Christmas wreath adorning his manly gift. For God, the boys in the locker room, and me to gander upon—snow balls anyone? It was endearingly funny, and, keeping the laughter inside, I chalked it up to the fact that he must have really loved me.

While dating Rebound, I realized I had not yet properly dealt with my feelings over the breakup with Six. Nor had I ever experienced any real or proper closure.

The result of my unfinished business came to the surface. I was with Rebound in Mammoth Mountain on a ski trip. With Rebound, we had to rent ski equipment, and the details of hitting the slopes are many when it comes to skiing. Rebound was a good sport, wanting to share the love I had for the mountain.

We were staying at my girlfriend's condo. It all felt too familiar for me as Mammoth was a place that held so many memories of Six, good and bad.

Rebound had a poor reaction to the altitude and became very ill. I looked at him and saw him as helpless. His white hair and skin blended together, too many shades of white coupled with a snowy backdrop.

Suddenly, I was missing the dark-haired, hot-headed, hot-blooded Latin.

What was wrong with me?

It took me half a day of constant work to pack the car and return his equipment. Rebound, lay in bed, suffering, as I readied the condo. I did it all, and, as I poured him into my car, I couldn't get us down from the mountain fast enough.

Rebound's illness and my awareness of my unfinished business with Six came to a head in my heart. It was time to leave behind all the white and figure out this mess I had made.

It took me what felt like forever to break away from Six, and now I was having to look closer at myself. It was an awful feeling. It was a sickening feeling. I felt like a crazy person making crazy choices that involved other people. There should be some sort of licensing for this type of behavior to protect the innocent. I was reckless with love and with the care of others' hearts.

Resurfacing issues beget unraveling, and I could not escape the process of pain. I had to face what I tried to avoid leaving my life behind with Six.

So, in very poor form, I broke it off with Rebound, to truly grieve over the one I needed to grieve over nearly a year earlier.

Crazy choices seemed to be my theme as I marched into more relationship insanity.

Grieving Over Six

"The time you spend grieving over a man should never exceed the amount of time you actually spent with him."

—Rita Rudner

C OMING TO GRIPS WITH SIX, THE MAN I BROKE UP WITH MONTHS earlier, was intense.

I feebly attempted to mend things with him.

He agreed to meet me at the beach; it was after sunset, late in winter. We sat in my car and talked, kissed, and cried. He was done with me and had moved on to another.

I was not stellar in the way I handled leaving our relationship, and I was paying the price now. I felt sick and wanted back all the familiarity of him, but once again, I was lost.

Six was still stinging from our ending but had found a gal that he matched with, and they were happy with their union. That evening, he was gracious to me. That evening he was tender to me.

I had to face my choices. It was time, I was overdue. I drove away from the beach parking lot knowing that our goodbye was now final.

So, I cried: dry-heaving, lying flat on my back on the floor, letting the pain pour out of me. I was down for days, and I couldn't see an end in sight. I took up residency in Pain Town; I staked out my territory in this Town and began building the foundations for my new sad home.

This grief process tore me up from the inside out. I sought the sweet relief of sleep but woke up every day to the same heart-wrenching sorrow. The floor was closer to the bottom—to the pit that was my life—so I stayed there, at odds with the bed that I looked up at, which was somehow out of reach. I didn't feel deserving of the comfort that was once my bed.

I thought I would die, but I did not. I wanted to die, but I did not.

It's hard to carry on with one's day when one goes through a break like this.

One of my friends used to always say, "Hey baby, go big or go home."

I went big and I was crashing big.

When people connect on an extreme level, there is a great deal that binds you. Routine, family unit, finances—even football season, or ski season—they become part of the spiritual cord that binds two people as one. It becomes difficult facing the everyday when what you once knew of every day goes away.

Somehow, I had to find a new normal. I had to find a new every day. Without Rebound Guy, and without familiar Six. I had to find a home and a routine in *me*.

What did that look like? I had no idea.

A voice inside my head that I refer to as "Spirit" beckoned me. Spirit said, "Go walk on the beach."

During what I call my mourning period, this voice was persistent.

"Go walk on the beach."

But my new residence on the floor was also persistent.

Mustering up courage, I dutifully obeyed the nagging voice inside my head and heart.

Pulling myself off the floor, I felt heavy. My legs ached and there was a hollowness behind my eyes. With dirty hair, baggy yoga pants, and a Beach Boy's t-shirt that I picked up at a concert when life was full of fun and hope fifteen years ago, my state of cleanliness was questionable.

My solution was to put my hair into a ponytail and douse my clothes with a squirt of Febreze air freshener as I passed by the laundry on the way to my car. I pushed my bedraggled, sorry self into my car, continuing to listen to Spirit as I headed to the beach.

I found it took a serious effort to even find a parking space. Suffering from head to toe, I felt the pain, but it seemed far off, as if I was not connected to my body.

After the long, brave, hesitant trek sauntering down the stairs that cascaded from the cliff to the sand, I found myself taking in the sounds and smells of the pounding surf. Being at the seaside can be a form of meditation, if I could just tune in.

Just a few short steps into my healing journey, I found a heart-shaped rock staring up at me from the promising sand, looking almost alone—separated from the other rocks—as if it was waiting. I picked it up and marveled at it.

"Okay, I get it," I told Spirit out loud, nodding my head at the treasure in my hand.

I will find my heart!

At this point in my life, my heart was very much lost. I didn't think it was possible to find it again, but Spirit obviously had other plans in store for me. This slowly brought me solace. I was alive.

As the ever-pounding tide continued, I kept breathing. The salty air entered my lungs, filling me with hope, and the mending process began. My fifty-first year was as much about healing as it was about finding myself. I put searching for the right man on hold to take time for myself.

I had a deep expectancy that things would get better and feel better. I was able to begin shifting out of my dark thoughts by finding things to be grateful for. Smiling through sadness, I began to experience the sensation of a genuine smile as I had before.

I hit the sand many times after that, finding a heart-shaped rock on each walk, and I always left with it nestled carefully inside my pocket. My heart was slowly finding its way back again.

Six is a passionate man, and I consider myself blessed that we shared the love we did. I think of him often and fondly, even while knowing with absolute certainty that I had to get out—I was fighting for my life. The light would have diminished from my eyes as I slowly evaporated had I stayed.

Six and I eventually reconnected as friends after we parted ways, and we will always have a certain love for one another. Honestly, it took years to reach that point, but we did.

Long after our breakup, there was a party at his parents' home. We started bickering like siblings who knew exactly which buttons to push to annoy one another. This was not attractive, yet it was a firm reminder of why we were no longer a couple.

After several margaritas, Six invited me to join him and his oldest daughter to go see his youngest daughter's rock band premiere.

Katie L. Lindley

Hopping into a bizarre time machine, the ticket for that ride was three shots of tequila.

Sitting in the back of an Escalade, getting cozy with one another, caused memories to flood back. How many years, months, and days had it been since we parted ways?

He smelled the same. He felt the same.

I was warm sitting next to him.

I had a temporary look back into the life I had left behind, the sweet part, forever missed and now revisited.

I will always love this man and his feisty brood.

BEEBE

"Walking with a friend in the dark is better than walking alone in the light."

—HELEN KELLER

DURING "THE BREAKUP," SIX AND I HAD OUR SEPARATE SET OF friends. Friends seemed to land on one side the fence or the other. It was quiet in my camp; I was the bad guy. Beebe was the only one who did not take "sides." Sometimes, it felt like I was losing more than a boyfriend, lover, and fiancé. I also lost most of the friends that surrounded us for years. Beebe never took sides and showed love to both Six and I at different times, like buddy-custody or a fifty-fifty split.

During the brief engagement with Six, I envisioned Beebe as my fiancé's best man, but truly I wanted him to be *my* best man. The three of us had shared many memorable moments together that were worth treasuring.

Once Six and I parted ways, Beebe and I became as thick as thieves. Our relationship went something like this: I'd be home in stretchy yoga clothes or oversized flannel pajamas and sitting on the couch having a bachelorette dinner of a glass of red wine, Have'A Corn Chips, and hummus. Then Beebe would send me a text.

"Hey BB, what are you doing?"

Note of clarification, he called me BB and I call him Beebe. Exact

85

same pronunciation, yet we both dutifully answered. A nickname only sticks if the other responds. This was our language we had with one another.

His text cued me to get off the couch. Before I could properly respond, I was already making my way upstairs, removing my clothes as I went. He was at a local bar and wanted my colorful company. I said *yes* to Beebe ninety-nine times out of one hundred, and off I would go. He is one of the dearest friends I have ever known. I am sure people saw us as a couple. Beebe liked to say it was just like we were married.

"We split meals and don't have sex," he would say, or "You are the best wife I'll never have."

He proclaimed me as his little sister, and I always knew he loved me. Dear Lord, I loved him. It had always been something special to have male friends I can count on that do not have a hidden naked agenda.

Beebe reminisced one time about his marriage and his ditzy ex-wife. She wanted to buy a Volvo, yet she pronounced it vulva. Beebe said, "No way am I going to have my wife call the dealership and say, 'My vulva needs servicing.' She can drive a Ford or a BMW, or a Chevy . . . but no way is she buying a Volvo."

You can see how he brought me belly laughter—the best medicine for any girl. He treated me like a queen: opened my door, pulled out my chair, paid for my meals, and always made me check in when I got home.

He was a King amongst men.

THE PIANO MAN

"I have a theory that the only original things we
ever do are mistakes."

—BILLY JOEL

ONE DAY, AS I MINDED MY OWN BUSINESS WHILE SHOPPING AT
the local Trader Joe's, I saw this very handsome man with a bright-
eyed two-year-old girl in his cart. I said to him, "You've got a long way
to go, mister."

He introduced himself to me as the Piano Player at The Montage.
The Montage is a very fancy hotel—the finest really, with an enchant-
ment setting that feels regal. He asked me to come visit him. He was so
cute that I thought he was flirting. However, his Southern charm and
mustering up business for himself factored in. One snag: he's married.
I don't visit, fraternize, or hang with married men. No thanks.

But then a few days later, there he was again. Then again, another
day when I went out to lunch, it was Piano Man that opened the door
with his charming, "Hello Miss."

This guy kept showing up like a bad habit with a Southern accent.
He greeted me with his Southern charm each time and asked, "Miss,
why haven't you come to see me at The Montage?"

I do not believe in coincidences—everything happens for a reason.
Piano Man kept gnawing at my thoughts. After all, he was popping

up around every corner. I wanted to find out why. It felt like there was a reason that I kept seeing him, one of those "Spirit" things I sometimes feel in my gut. I finally came up with a solution. Beebe would accompany me to see Piano Man play.

It didn't take much to convince Beebe to join me, and off we went to the lovely Montage. It was about seven thirty, and the Piano Man did not start until eight. Beebe and I settled in with a bottle of wine at a table while we waited. Beebe and I were having such a good time. We rocked to the tunes as Piano Man belted out some favorites like *California Dreaming* and *Candle in the Wind*. It was summertime, and I was wearing a long blue summer dress that seemed to match the ocean. I felt so blissful and free that night, just like a candle in the wind.

Beebe said, off-the-cuff, with Cabernet leading the conversation, "Hey, you love to wheel and deal . . . go see how much you can get us a room for and we'll party all night long."

I took this as a challenge and marched up to the front desk and asked for the manager.

"My friend and I are locals, we're not even lovers, we just want to party and stay the night." I, of course, offered more information than necessary.

The manager replied, "The rooms start at seven-hundred and fifty," but he was willing to let one go for four-fifty.

I thanked him and strolled back to deliver the pricey news to Beebe.

"See if you can get him down to three hundred."

Meeting the challenge with glee, I made my way back to the manager as if to close a deal with some high-stake significance.

I squared off, asking, "How about three hundred?"

The manager said, "Three-fifty."

I smacked my hand down like a flying gavel on the granite desk and said, "Alright then yes, I'll tell my friend."

I bounced back to the table with a renewed spring in my step. I informed Beebe. "Go get us checked in, please," I joyfully requested, full of red wine and with a dimpled smile.

The Montage had a magic of its own. I marveled at the perfectly polished marble floors and high-vaulted ceilings. Everywhere I looked, there was another detail of the finest quality. The lobby smelled like fresh flowers, and, as you stepped on the balcony, a whiff of salt air accompanied the sound of the pounding surf. The Montage had strung lights in between two palm trees that gave you the sense of a moon just for them. Of course, if there was the possibility of two moons, one might show up here.

Beebe and I continued to listen to Piano Man, had more wine, and danced a little. Piano Man sat down with us and chatted us up between sets. He seemed very outgoing and was well suited to be in the public eye as he entertained with ease and talent. I was happy to get to know this pleasant man who constantly bragged about his family. With his dimpled cheeks and Southern drawl, who wouldn't like this charmer?

I felt like I landed in a fairytale, just like Cinderella after midnight. I was ready to find my pumpkin and head back to the castle. Feeling the effects of too much wine and too little food, it was time to go to our room. Beebe offered me his arm as we made our way through the breathtaking resort. Heels clicking on the fancy Italian marble floors, it was spectacular.

Awaiting us were some fresh chocolates with Beebe's last name somehow written in delicious goo. The huge porcelain tub was calling me, and I made myself right at home, filling up the warm water and climbing in. Beebe came into the bathroom, which was larger than my bedroom, because I left the door wide open. I am not shy, and taking up modesty with my best friend wasn't part of my personality. I leaned forward toward my legs, exposing my back. I looked up at him and handed him a washcloth. He obliged and began to scrub my awaiting pink and glistening back, with great sweetness.

Afterward, I floated about like a mermaid in the large tub with three strategically placed washcloths on my body as we chatted. There are moments when time stalls; this was one of them. We yammered on like friends do until I was as wrinkled as a prune. Eventually he left me alone again so I could get ready for bed in privacy.

I found Beebe sitting on the deck in his very fine Montage bathrobe, listening to the pounding surf, watching the moon over the water. It was a glorious evening with a sight to behold. I felt minor panic rise inside as I imagined him swan-diving off the deck onto the cold, perfectly-laid brick sidewalk. I insisted he come inside. He laughed and told me, "Leave me alone, woman, I just want my balls in the breeze."

"I'm not going to be able to fall asleep worrying about you outside," I said, sounding way too much like a nagging wife, or worse, a mom.

He gave up his ball-moment when he saw I was worried about him. I'll never understand what it is like to have balls in the breeze. I regretted not leaving him alone in his much-deserved man time.

We melted, sinking deep into our separate beds dressed in their finest linens and bedding, fit for a king or queen.

"Oh Lord," I thought as I drifted off to sleep, "I hope he doesn't tell Six!" Hell, why should I care? At the very least Beebe should be able to leave with a bit of bragging rights. We did not have sex then, or ever in our friendship for that matter, but what we shared was a very special and memorable fairytale night. The last thing I would want to do is muck up our friendship with sex.

HOMIES IN THE HOOD

"I was raised in a Baptist household, went to a Catholic church, lived in a Jewish neighborhood, and had the biggest crush on the Muslim girls from one neighborhood over."

—WILL SMITH

A COUPLE OF DAYS LATER, WHILE I DROVE THROUGH THE NEIGH-borhood I had lived in for over twenty-odd years, there was Piano Man. Standing in his front yard, coffee in hand, surrounded by his white picket fence, minding his own business. Turned out, he's a neighbor. I pulled over to say hello. He was full of his never-boring Southern charm. I thanked him for insisting I come visit him at the Montage and told him how Beebe and I had a wonderful time. We chatted for a moment and I mentioned to him I was trying to find a rental home for my parents. Piano Man said his wife was a real estate agent. He ran into his home and grabbed a couple of her cards. No wonder I kept running into this man, we lived blocks away and swam in the same circles.

I called his beautiful wife because I needed real estate advice. That same day, I was invited to her and Piano Man's home, where she and I embarked on a real estate journey. Once I saw her sparkling blue eyes, I knew she was going to be just as charming as Piano Man. She was just the person I needed to meet at that point in my life. Piano Man's wife guided me for days on end. We went from address to address in order to find the right home for my parents.

The first time we hopped in her car, she immediately took a wrong turn and said, "Shit!"

The sound of her potty mouth made me fall in love with her as well. She literally had me at "shit." She quickly became my newest best gal pal. Thank you, Piano Man. I love Mrs. Piano Man!

As for the toddler in Piano Man's Trader Joe's shopping cart—well, guess who ended up referring to me as "Auntie?" I decided to give them my childhood piano, which was gathering dust at my house. Ironic that my piano ended up in Piano Man's family, as it should be. This way, his sweet daughter could grow up with Daddy playing the piano at home.

I began babysitting this rapidly growing, blue-eyed, blonde doll, who liked to be a princess one moment and Batman the next. Being around her made me look forward to grandchildren one day. I believe that serendipitous fate had a guiding hand in bringing our lives together. I know I am meant to interact with the people I meet and come across each day, and I am grateful for that. My friends and family always serve as a mirror to help me to better understand myself. And Beebe and I will always have our shared exquisite night at the Montage.

ONCE AGAIN

"If at first you don't succeed, find out if the loser gets anything."

—WILLIAM LYON PHELPS

I FOUND MYSELF AT THE SAME PLACE I WAS AT BEFORE I MET SIX; I had more than one man filling my days. My phone was ringing off the hook, with an old buddy who wanted to chat about his girlfriend on the other end. Then I'd meet Beebe in the harbor for lunch, later rounding off my evening with dinner and a movie with a potential new boyfriend that I had met online.

Was it familiarity that sent me back into "a man for every purpose," or was it something else? No one needed four pairs of black pumps and twelve pairs of shoes. Yet my shoe closet was, once again, chalk-full. I wanted one dependable, long-wearing shoe that I could slip into every season and introduce to my family.

Katie L. Lindley

MAN OH MEN

"One's philosophy is not best expressed in words;
it is expressed in the choices one makes ... and the
choices we make are ultimately our responsibility."
—ELEANOR ROOSEVELT

The whirlwind of my dating adventures had given me motion sickness. There were so many men out there for me to meet. Tall, short, wealthy, struggling, happy, confused, bitter, berated, quirky, the list goes on and on. I had to face it: if I was in a life transition, then so was my next date.

Are men really that different than I am? I had to figure out what I was looking for and what worked for me.

Was I looking for the protector? The shoulder to lean on? To make me feel like I am the one and only, being treated like the Queen to his Kingdom? I did believe there was a good man out there for me ... attempting to hold my crown firmly in place.

To match up with someone online, or elsewhere, a multitude of factors come into play. It seems I had a tendency to repeat relationship patterns. How do I break the cycle of the ineffective? Repeating vicious relationship cycles is simply not healthy. Doing the same thing over and over while expecting a different result could be seen as insanity of the heart. In theory, taking a break from men and reflecting on myself seemed to be in order. It was high time to grow up and learn how I was affecting my outcomes and misgivings in romantic relationships.

So, I did just the opposite: I acquired a friend with benefits.

Friend With Benefits

"When I did 'Sex and the City,' it was like, 'Let's do a comedy where the humor is not coming from innuendo but from a truthful place. This is a show where we're going to be able to say and do what we want.'"

—Darren Star

That's when the universe ordered me up some sex. And that so-called sex really changed my preconceived ideas about how things should be.

I took on a friend with benefits. He was a single healthy man who was in no shape for a relationship but was in great shape for lovemaking. Undoubtedly, I was the same shape because that was what I got, law of manifestation. It was my suggestion that we become bang buddies, and in record speed he was at my doorstep, duh. We kissed and fumbled our way upstairs, uttering the rules of our relationship. I was notably nervous. Seems he was a bit more experienced at this type of deal than I was. Here I go again trying something new.

He said to me, "Sweetheart, making love for the first time can be nerve-wracking."

That smooth comment alone should have signaled that he had had many first times.

It was late in the morning and the room was drenched in sunlight. I remember this as a moment where darkness and a soft candle would have served me. We were like two high school kids when the parents were gone. When I saw him buck naked, I thought, "Oh, holy cow! Thank God for the coconut oil, now where is the shoehorn?" Panic and excitement riveted through my body. For me, getting out of my head and into the moment of pleasure could be a gap. Yoga, meditation and being present helped. I tried letting go of misconstrued ideas and allowed myself to receive. These things were vital if one wanted to pass Sex 101.

Did I just think this guy was great because I had been without sex for far too long? He showed me that sex could look so much differently than anything I had ever known. He took his time. I mean, really took his time. My previous experiences had shown me the twenty minutes, orgasm, done. With Benefit, twenty minutes was just getting warmed up.

However, we never had great passion, you know, the tear-your-clothes-off deal. Our sexual encounters were always pre-ordered, respectful, and polite. He was a by-product of Viagra. It was obvious but never spoken, the blue pill had to be invited to the party. The comfort level was through the roof. God forbid I should ever become Mrs. Benefit, uh no! I was gently forcing a new sexual situation that seemed right at the time, but was it?

The rules for friends with benefits seem to differ between each relationship. They are ever-changing depending on individual needs and/or comfort levels. Our particular relationship took different forms. Knowing he was on a dating frenzy, I seemed to attach more rules in a feeble attempt to gain control. I tried cornering him for more attention, and that in no way worked. The sex was going to be what it was. Too bad I could really never get the hang of that type of setup.

Benefit and I did have tender moments, or so I thought. This had been perplexing, and I ran through the gamut of emotions with this liaison. Eventually, and somewhat heartbreakingly so, I understood that I'm not the casual sex kind of a girl. I wanted to think of myself as free and brave, but I'm not. I'm the girl that gets caught up in believing that "happily ever after" may somehow be linked to my vagina. I've got to stop watching chick flicks.

Benefit, well, he was just a bang buddy. I was clearly sliding down a slippery slope in a direction that did not suit me. That being said, I evolved and changed through this like never before. I broke through the ceiling of limitations of how sex had to present itself and what it was supposed to look like. Love and sex are not scripted as in the movies; they are written on our hearts. Sex and love do not have to go hand in hand. This is a lie I have battled for years. For me to experience this type of freedom caused me to drop judgment on other people's love, or sex life. Many of my married girl friends were lacking when it came to sex with their husbands. With my bang buddy, I was getting my needs met. Benefit did so much for me, it was truly groundbreaking.

In some regard, I must admit, I benefited from Benefit.

I Would Like To Order One Man With A Side Of Fidelity

"Histories are more full of examples of the fidelity of dogs than of friends."

—Alexander Pope

ONE SATURDAY NIGHT, BENEFIT ASKED IF WE COULD "GET TOgether" after his drink date with another girl. Therein lies the problem; Benefit is quite the lady's man. He asked me to have a glass of wine in anticipation of us being "together" later that evening. That sounded like a grand idea, however, I forgot to factor in that he was on a date. I was two glasses in, and he was two hours late.

I signed back up for online dating as I waited for a man that was out with another woman. I probably shouldn't have posted photos and written about myself when it was late and I had wine pulsing through my veins while my bang buddy was indifferent. Lo and behold, I was back and in the shark tank. Strap on your snorkel gear, little trooper, I was back actively online, swimming towards I don't know what.

I was trying at all lengths to avoid being the proverbial girl that sat at home on a Saturday night, but I was failing. The Beach Boys said don't leave your best girl home on a Saturday night. I wasn't his best girl, not even close, and that was the problem. I was no one's best girl.

I thought casual sex was easy—I was being more physically satisfied than my married friends, right? But I guess deep down I knew it wasn't for me. My experience with Benefit pushed me to want a more solid relationship with someone who wanted the same. Perhaps a guy who wanted me for simple things like hanging out, walks on the beach... oh Good Lord, I sound like a please-date-me ad. You know what I meant—a guy who's into me.

So simple, right?

Benefit and I happily remained friends as the benefit part ended with very little drama. Of course it did, he could replace me in a moment's notice and probably did.

That brief friends with benefits experiment went rather well. It was a journey of self-discovery, I suppose. Although it was something I tried on, with me, this arrangement simply did not fit!

Blind Dating Or Dating Blindly

"I've been on so many blind dates, I should get a free dog."

—Wendy Liebman

I WAS FRESHLY FIFTY-TWO AND DONE WITH THE CASUAL SEX THING; it was time to give online dating another try.

Computer dating is like standing in the middle of a candy store on a hot afternoon after going to an amusement park all day. Your blood sugar is dropping whilst you contemplate adrenaline rush verses nausea. Never-ending choices that all look so possible. It can really spin your head.

The more I looked at all of these successful online couplings, the more I wondered, what's wrong with me? When did dating get to be so complicated? You have to factor in so many rules; let them chase you, do not give away sex too soon or they will lose interest. The rules of dating, the feng shui of dating, and clear out the old, get ready for the new. Dating soulmates from past lives—oh dear Lord, would someone buy me a drink and take me to the backseat of his car?

Online dating rules are so constraining. When can I just be the spectacular girl I've convinced myself that I am?

OREGON GUY

"Think left and think right and think low and think high. Oh, the thinks you can think up if only you try!"

—Dr. Seuss

DATING ONLINE EXPANDS OUR POSSIBILITIES FAR BEYOND WHAT one would think. It's highly unlikely that I would have met Oregon Guy any other way. I mean we were a thousand miles apart. I reached out to him as soon as I saw his location and photo.

"One of my best girlfriends lives in Eugene," I emailed him on the dating site.

I have never bantered back and forth with anyone like this man. He ran circles around words. We hit it off and began a phone relationship with off the charts laughter and continued repartee with no end in sight.

We both really liked each other. I believe that was where we went wrong.

Or, where I went wrong.

Our phone friendship had reached the level that it was time to meet. I had many friends in Oregon and it was easy for me to buy a ticket, stay with them, and meet my new Oregon Guy. This was all wrapped up in a discounted plane ticket. Oregon Guy, of course, was scheduled to meet me at the airport.

Katie L. Lindley

When one meets face to face, so many factors take place all at once. Body language, energy, chemistry, all firing at lightening speeds yet undetectable as we feebly attempt to sort through what our brain is registering. We both had tremendous anticipation for the great airport scene. It should have been in black and white, with the clicking of the film reel sounding in the background, fading to curtains billowing in the breeze. I think a crackling fireplace is in that shot?

My romantic expectations were too high. Instead, our meeting moment unfolded in color, in reality, with nervous tension ever present. I had airplane hair and a primal nervous smell coming from my armpits. He was a real gentleman in every sense of the word, but I did not make the chemistry connection with him I had hoped to. In hindsight, I'm aware that anticipation, riddled with excitement and daunting fear bundled all together, played their part. Another dumb lesson in learning to take my time with love. Damn, once again, damn.

Oregon Guy was a man amongst men. Though my nerves were wracked when I met him face-to-face, I knew how wonderful he was. After time passed, I pushed for friendship. Being the gracious dude he was, he accepted. Lucky me! Weeks later, we were chatting on the phone, and he suggested I put a couple of my photos together for a commercial that he was producing. I thought of this as rather ridiculous but threw my hat, or pictures taken from my mobile phone, into the arena. How many years had it been since I modeled, a decade times two?

Lights, Camera, Action...

"I'm not that good-looking . . . nobody is that good-looking. I have seen a lot of movie stars, and maybe four are amazing looking. The rest have a team of gay guys who make it happen."
—Tina Fey

RECEIVING THE PHONE CALL FROM THE CASTING AGENCY, I DID my best to remain cool. They inquired if I had an agent—uh, no, huh, not so much. Let the acting begin! I remained calm as if this was a normal, everyday conversation for me. So, yippee, I got a job in Oregon. I began jumping around in my room yelping out a woohoo or two. I have never been shy, and the thought of being in front of the camera thrilled me to no end. Of course, I laughed my ass off, dancing alone in my bedroom, the moment I hung up the phone with the nice gentleman that was graciously making my arrangements.

I proceeded to get as done up as possible with hydrating facials, Botox for my wrinkles, French manicure and pedicure on my nails, and color for my hair. I was ravishing, darling. Made up like Orange County women do. Perfectly natural, uh, but not really.

I was thrilled over the moon when I met my handsome cast husband. I thought, "Oh goody, this would be easy."

Easy it was. He was a dream; he had been in the business for thirty years and was a delight. Married, with three small children. He guided me along with what was important in the made-up world in front of the cameras; remove all egos, show up on time, do what is asked the best you can, never care if they use you or not. It is about the paycheck. What a great way to get paid! For me, it was a fantasy. Ironically the only suggestion from the director during filming was, "you don't have to touch him so often." Up to this point in my life, that was the most exciting way to work. I would sign up for it again.

I was able to spend time with my Oregon Guy, hammering out what conspired between us. We headed back to Portland together and had truly bonded. I was sensitive, knowing he had unfinished business with me. I am aware that was why I got the job. This was a reminder to handle love with consideration; treat everyone in a gracious fashion.

Weeding through all the wrong guys online was worth it because I very much adore Oregon Guy. We laugh our butts off, sharing horror stories about our dating mishaps. Tongue in cheek, we have coined online dating as Mismatch, Disharmony, Plenty of Fucks, and Sixty Shades of Dating, having an ongoing love/hate relationship with on-line possibilities.

STAR DRESSER

"The fault . . . is not in our stars, But in ourselves."
—WILLIAM SHAKESPEARE, JULIUS CAESAR

I SAT GLEEFULLY LISTENING TO PIANO MAN AT THE LOVELY Montage, as I did once every couple of months, accompanied by the beautiful Mrs. Piano Man. In walked a television commercial executive producer and his sidekick—the costume wardrobe guy for film and TV. The wardrobe guy had worked on such films as Twilight, Mr. and Mrs. Smith, and Marie Antoinette. He has dressed celebrities such as Angelina Jolie and Julia Roberts. I call him Star Dresser.

He was acclaimed for styling the costume to fit the character. And of course, he was no less than well put together himself. He was very handsome; he kind of reminded me of a young Richard Gere.

I was feeling the effects of my two martinis and boldly asked him, "Are you gay?"

That seemed like a reasonable question.

His eyes smiled as he politely said, "No."

A moment later, on a roll with my Tourette's mouth, I told him, "Oh! You should come help me organize my clothes."

How outlandish of me! His friend chimed in and matched my boldness by saying, "Yeah, he'll do your closet if you'll do him."

Really, dude? I retorted, "I would not have sex, but I would make you dinner."

I glanced at handsome Star Dresser, resorting to my familiar mom card.

I had a great evening, but, after that night, I never gave a second thought to these two gentlemen.

A couple of weeks later, out of the blue, Star Dresser sent me a text saying that he was in town and ready to go through my closet. I was floored! I was completely confused why he would do something for me, a total stranger. I was thrilled at the whole idea nonetheless, so I jumped on it.

It was a hurried, full day, and I just had time to pick up the dirty underwear from my floor and take a quick bath. I was well aware that I would be trying on clothes, so contemplating what type of panties was a serious and thoughtful consideration. My best, newest bra of course, properly fitting and not squeezing excess back skin—never a good look. I realized granny panties were a big no, as was a thong. I choose something in-between the two; a sassy little boy-short panty that was fairly new and impressively clean. I was shaved where it counted, and I set aside the fact that my weight was not at the sweet spot. Appreciating my body was *way* more important than how I looked.

For some reason unbeknownst to me, I said exactly what was on my mind with Star Dresser. He got out of his car, and I took one look at him and said out loud for God and my neighbors to hear, "Oh, damn, you are so cute."

The words hung in the air as my mouth gaped open. This time I saw a bit of Brad Pitt in him. A chameleon of good-looking men.

He easily managed where brave men didn't dare go, he had me undressed at "hello." Of course, this was his job and I was comfortable with that. There could be no embarrassment with Star Dresser or I would be sunk. We took a shot of tequila and then ran upstairs. Clothes were flying within moments, although his stayed on. This event was life-altering for me. Getting rid of what I no longer needed and clearing space for what I actually used was amazing. Donating clothes to those who could use them continued my high. I rid myself of armpit-stained white shirts I should have felt embarrassed to wear and should have abandoned years ago.

I felt revitalized. I realized I did not need to go shopping; my closet was rather complete. The need for "more" become less important. I began clearing out further clutter that had been slowing down my life. I felt lighter, liberated, and full of potential. I became aware of how heavy holding onto past things made me feel. By clearing my life of material clutter, I was trying to clear my heart for new possibilities.

Star Dresser reads scripts and people. He loves what he does. When you think about it, we are constantly presenting ourselves. No matter if we are going to the market, carpool, a long walk, yoga class, or church, the clothes we wear speak volumes on how we feel about ourselves.

Seemingly glancing into one's soul, Star Dresser can put together the "look" that reflects the "lifestyle." He is brilliant at what he does. His skills factor in so many things at one time. A great deal of intuition, like a good cop or a shrink, putting together the personality profile that matches the clothes. His take of me was a free-spirited, earthy yoga chick, that in a pinch can pull off a James Bond's date look. I'd like to think his perception of me was spot on.

After hours of sorting through what was not appropriate, or my style, or in style, we made headway.

He would say, "I never want to see you in this," or, "This is not you," or, "This Kardashian look should never be pulled off, even by them."

My favorite was, "Just because you *can* wear this doesn't mean you *should*."

The pile of "never again" clothes on the floor formed a small, yet substantial, mountain. Hiking over it would require a parking pass and water.

I was giddy, running around in my scanties. It was well after midnight when I finally kicked my new friend out. I walked him to his car and we shared a passionate tequila-motivated kiss. He may have tossed me on the hood of his car … it all became blurry. Wasn't he Italian? He kissed like he was French, oh la la.

After a while, I got the gist of what worked for me and what didn't. My car was packed full of donations; someone who could use my clothes, that felt good. Star Dresser's words ran through my head every damn time I got dressed, be it good or bad. He was brilliant when it came to putting looks together. I have always been a clothes hound—I have clothes for every occasion. When a guy asks me out and tells me what we will be doing, my mind goes to my closet, runs through the inventory, and I figure out what I will wear as "yes" comes from my lips. Beach, boating, concert, ballgame—I have the looks for all events.

Apparently, I was a clothes hoarder as well.

Never again. Star Dresser taught me the valuable lesson of letting go. We never became intimate, but I am well aware Star Dresser changed my life. A very handsome wardrobe angel.

Katie L. Lindley

Getting my closets in order had a snowball effect on me as I began to get my whole house and life in order! Artwork I had painted, that had been sitting around for dozens of years collecting dust, was gone by the end of the week. I purged, and it felt great; clearing out the old and preparing for possibilities of the new.

I was so very grateful to Star Dresser and what he had done for me, and, half kidding, I suggested we start a business together. Saving the world one closet at a time! Good thing I kept my Batman undies!

Dirty Little Secret

"The captain requests that you please keep your seatbelt fastened while you are in your seat. The plane may experience unexpected turbulence."
—Any Flight Attendant

I FIND IT INTERESTING THAT WHEN I MEET SOMEONE AND HIT IT off with ease how days can turn into weeks and then into months. Time flies by. It was going on five months of time flying by. I had been dating this man that shall remain even more nameless than the other men.

Dirty Little Secret is a businessman, a pillar in his wealthy conservative community, and all-around great guy, and a stellar single dad. You get the picture; he's one of the good ones. Yes, ladies, there are good guys out there.

We met standing in line at a coffee shop in Newport Beach. He chatted me up and we had coffee together. That was our first date.

He is a tallish, boyish, blond-haired "fox." He had the dude-next-door looks as well as a lean, tight body. I was fifty-three and he had just turned fifty.

He would not allow me to carry my wallet, because when we were together, it was his treat. It was a treat for me to spend time with Dirty Little Secret for sure. I understood men could be considerate daters, but this one was even more insistent on the order that the courting process should take place. We would drink too many margaritas and laugh for hours. His well-honed skill of making margaritas included taking grapefruit off his tree and squeezing the life out of it to add to this heavenly concoction. His keen sense of humor, along with his outgoing personality, was a great fit for me. I was falling in love, not the instant kind, but the type of love that eventually sneaks up on you. Bam!

We would walk his dog to the beach and talk about a future together. He told me stories of when he was a pilot and the crazy nights he had flying amongst the stars. He wanted a boat so we could anchor off the coast and lay under the same set of stars together. We would stay up late and watch horrible B movies just to mock them to no end. We did the kind of stuff that is romantic and memorable. It seemed so ideal, with a proper amount of sweetness.

Oh, but not so fast … before I sent out wedding invites, there was one glitch. Yes, there was just one thing missing, uh …sex. We managed to confirm the relationship naked, but it was without great fanfare and lacking in that certain spark. I wondered if he found me attractive, and I began to question my own sexuality. Still, there was enough good between us, so I efficiently batted it away into a little place I call "denial."

He explained that he had had a delicate scrotum surgery for a health issue that left him not responding the same way sexually. Okay, I could understand that. He was such a stand-up man, and I wasn't going to disregard him due to a lack of desire or full ability.

Feeling supportive and optimistic about what we had, I focused on the positive. With great measure on his part, he finally introduced me to his sons and his sister. Things were looking good. His business was picking up, and he bought himself a new Porsche that he paid for in cash. Dirty Little Secret's first stop was my house to take me out for a spin. There is something about that new car smell, coupled with the speed and sound of the engine, that turns me on. He may not be doing it for me in the bedroom, but this car did it for me on the road. I have always fancied cars; I'm my father's daughter. Give me a swanky upscale car with a big engine and great brakes. I drive cars hard and love the power of a good ride. Damn!

We would drive his new car up and down the Pacific Coast Highway early Sunday mornings to check out the surf and get coffee. Cars and coffee, that was his deal. He was the guy who knew all the guys everywhere we went. When we were in his town, we always ran into someone he knew. I was his sassy sidekick. It was like dating the town mayor;

always a baby to kiss, an old woman to help cross the street. Anytime we ventured out of town for the day, it was sweet just to be with him.

Things were comfortable between us and I felt calm with him. However, a relationship that was absent of sex started to confuse me. The fact that it was not present was challenging to ignore. I talked to a couple of my friends that have put sex on the shelf. This is something I never recommend—I believe sex is to be enjoyed, a vital part of coupling. Yet, here I was, enjoying a man without the sex. I did consider taking a lover but was conflicted with the idea. I chose to stay in this relationship, and, when most necessary, have my way with myself.

Was I choosing to put aside what mattered to me? Compromising myself once again?

After several months, things seemed to be picking up. He felt excited about his future and put me in all of his future dreams. I saw myself as Mrs. Dirty Little Secret. It was a safe, peaceful existence, filled with fast cars and stars, and somehow a boat came into our vision as well.

Our physical connection went as far as midnight spooning. This seemed to fill me up for the moment.

We never spent any substantial amount of time together in a row. Consecutive time together allows for bonding and continuity. The fact that it was absent nagged at me. I mean, if I was his forever-after-babe, shouldn't we spend three days in a row together? At least?

I mentioned this to him, insistent that this was what we needed to do next. There I went again, trying to take back some kind of control. I hate that I did that, but I did. I liked defined plans, and I grabbed for order far too often. It's a lesson that kept repeating—I had to let go of things, like Star Dresser taught me. Trying to put into sequence how a relationship should go is fruitless. It is far more important to love myself and understand the happiness I had at that moment.

The little "A" type in me that tried to forever control life around me won out, and I boldly suggested we spend a week together. (Seriously, a whole week). What was I thinking?! We had never even spent an entire weekend together. I was full of brass. Or lacking in common sense. Or once again desperate for that happy ending.

His response was a photo of his bed with leather straps perfectly anchored at the four corners.

The text read, "Do you still want to spend a week with me?"

I admit this threw me off. This was happening over text, so I had a few moments to compose my wild, unending thoughts. Thank God. What I knew for sure: I liked him, he had been so very kind to me. I didn't judge and I was a big girl. I wrote about sex and openly talked about it, so I needed to have a big girl response.

It all made sense. He was attracted to me, but he had his fetish and I was not a part of that. I wondered, "Could I give it a college try?"

The next day he called with an awkward, louder-than-usual, "Hello."

His hello kind of jumped at me. He made himself vulnerable to share this side of himself with me, and I thankfully mustered up grace toward him.

"Well, hello to you." Cheerful response on my part, check. Remain cool, be the cool chick, I reminded myself.

"So, what do you think?" he said.

"I have one question," I said.

"I bet you have a thousand."

"I do, but I'm only going to ask you one. I could come up with dozens, but most of them are none of my business."

He replied, "Okay … what is it?"

He was bracing himself, I was sure.

"Why did it take you this long to tell me?"

That was all I asked him.

I bargained with myself. Had he snuck it on me in a romantic way, it may have been an adventure. I felt somehow betrayed, as if I was worthy of his love but not his trust. I wondered if I was significant enough for him to fully expose himself to me, and did I count? Why was he compelled to keep this part of himself from me? Or worse, maybe he didn't find me sexy?

"I didn't think you were that kind of a girl, and I didn't want to scare you off."

"Well, I'm not a prude. I am not judgmental . . . I do trust you."

I basically told him to bring it on.

I was somewhat relieved that his secret was out. I didn't take the lack of our sex personally anymore. With the excitement of the unknown, I went bra shopping to try and show my full support by purchasing a black strappy number with panties to match. I looked like I was ready for the modest cover of "S&M Monthly."

The next time I saw Dirty Little Secret, I had the back of my dress halfway unzipped so he could catch a glimpse of the saucy bra I was wearing.

He asked me, "Do you want me to guide you into the restaurant backward?"

He was funny but did not understand my fashion statement. There goes a hundred bucks and change. We did not strap down that night.

The next morning, he said, "I am just considering all of this, so many things to factor in."

That, I agreed with.

I told him, "I don't want you to feel as if I'm a compromise. I don't want to be anyone's compromise. I want you to know complete happiness, and if this is what you want . . . I want you to have a full life."

I was not saying goodbye to him, but somehow it stood as our goodbye moment. I wish I had known that then, I would have held him longer and stayed in that place next to him that made me feel so safe.

Dirty Little Secret never did take me on his special sexual journey, but I imagine it was for the best. Our time together was but a few months. Bottom line, I am the girl who wants to be touched, told how pretty she is, and how much she is loved. I am not looking to be in a wild scene from a movie, or a staged, well-orchestrated act.

BIG

"Never give up on what you really want to do. The person with the BIG dreams is more powerful than the one with all the facts."

—JACKSON BROWN, JR.

THANK GOD FOR "SEX IN THE CITY" BECAUSE NO OTHER DESCRIP-tion would fit this man. I would very much like to use the word big a thousand times in a row, being painfully redundant. He had a big house, big job, big accomplishments, big dreams, and big blue eyes. I even had a big reaction when I met him.

We met at an online site. Deciding that a sushi fusion restaurant would be a great fit for our first date, he sat at the corner of the bar waiting for me. He had such a presence that I liked him right away.

We both were at the onset of a cold. Big gallantly ran next door to the pharmacy to get me magical Flu Away, an over-the-counter med-icine. He had me at cold medicine; maybe I'm too easy? Just writing about him makes my heart swell. I recently heard that we cannot choose who we fall in love with. Or can we?

Big had a full head of hair he dyed dark brown. It did not quite fit with his age, almost sixty, but in Newport Beach this was quite the standard. The only problem with his dyed hair was the white hair on his chest. With a mind of their own, the white chest hairs would curl their way out of his shirts.

Katie L. Lindley

Going exactly opposite of not trying to make over men, which I recommend, I forged ahead. I gently led him to shaving the lot off so I no longer felt distracted by the wandering silver hairs I wanted to pluck right off his body with my bare hands. The weirdest things make me crazy.

As a result of falling for him, though it was too soon, I hid my profile from the online dating site. I mean, I was hook, line, and sinker for this newly hairless-chested man.

Every corner of Big's home was immaculate and luxe. Seven bathrooms seemed excessive, however, I used six out of the seven. Seven, really? One for each day of the week? Oh no, it's Tuesday! The Tuesday issued-bathroom is the one up the hall, three doors on the left.

The smell of opulence hung in the air. Decorated to the nines, I felt at home while walking through his palace like the queen of the castle. I surely had my way in his kitchen, complete with a professional stove top, two sinks, and two dishwashers. The best news was that when we cooked up a feast he ran around after me, sponge in hand. The smile on his face told me he was delighted by our kitchen performance. We were having big fun.

One evening, we were sitting in his back-house watching a movie. The back-house sat on top of the garage. You could reach it from the stairs by the kitchen, or walk across a deck that hosted all sorts of seating alongside a barbecue and piped-in sound system that lead to the master suite, and a water view of Balboa Bay.

As we were intertwined on his comfy couch, approved by Restoration Hardware, Pottery Barn, or any second or first-rate decorator, he held my hand and heavily insinuated promises of a future. I do believe he meant it at that exact moment in time.

He said to me, "Four and four."

He said what now?

"What four horses and four dogs would you like us to have on my Montana property?"

I wanted to marry him right on the spot. I needed no other information. That sounded like a perfect endgame to me, painting the picture of our animal family. I had happily ever after all planned out, down to the breeds of said beasts and where we would live. I knew exactly what breeds, the names of each animal. I kept my mouth shut, but my head said, "Georgie and Farley, Cooper, oh, and Frankie…" I felt like a nine-year-old that just got her first collector's edition Barbie. *Dreams really do come true!*

He said it; I misread it, and I wanted to misread it. Happily ever after on a beautiful stead, both man and horse. Uh, yes, I'm in. This was as good as any proposal I could hear.

Uh, *maybe not.*

There was something big between this man and me, and I knew it. However, he had skillfully kept me at arm's length. He pulled me in, and I would easily show up. Then, politely, he pushed me away, sending me running off in the opposite direction.

So, despite what I told myself was a proposal, my heart knew better. I convinced myself that because we were woven together forever, we should be together. I had to stop thinking like that. I chose a man that was halfway in, and that's what I got—half a boyfriend. Looking for another half of a guy seemed tricky, yet I knew a ton of half men that were ready and willing.

We had the tear-your-clothes-off-on-the-stairs chemistry. Big and I never had the "talk," the one that leads to an exclusive relationship. However, I believed we were sexually exclusive.

I was so blindly naive, and this innocence was not serving me. Time to have a chat with myself. If I wanted to play with the big boys, I'd better figure out the rules. Maybe with a half boyfriend I should only get half-naked? I was clearly feeling half-crazed.

This was where Big turned into the villain/hero that we love to hate and hate to love. I sensed that he was, in fact, a busy boy on his dating site. I pulled up my site to check on him, and lo and behold, not only was his profile online, he was online at that exact moment.

Ditch the guy, right?

I struggled with that, and, indeed, called him out on it. I jumped on the phone, angry in my own delusion, he handled me with kid gloves and set up a date for the following Friday night. I accepted his invitation and started to calm down.

In hindsight, buttoning my pie hole would have served me better. If I didn't know what to say and was reacting out of sheer fear or anger, I needed to learn how to wait. I appeared insecure. I could have handled that conversation better.

"Girl, give yourself a moment—don't react," I thought. Wait twenty-four hours until you are settled down. After all, Big was Big long before I got there, and now I needed to just breathe.

My Choices With Big

"Make bold choices and make mistakes. It's all those things that add up to the person you become."

—Angelina Jolie

After I knew Big was still hunting online, I was willing to accept him for what he was. Also, I needed time to try and sort out what we were. Or moreover how I was feeling.

Our time together, though irregular, was sweet and engaging. Bedtime routine included a familiar Jacuzzi bath that could fit four people. His bathroom would have made Hugh Hefner proud. I giggled one more time as I plopped onto his insanely comfortable king-sized bed. I exhaled deeper than I had at any moment in the day. Okay, all was good, I was happy and he was not pushing me to watch the Camelot series on conspiracy theories, UFOs, or better yet, Area 51. All interesting topics, however, sometimes a girl just wants to relax and not contemplate the unseen dangers of the universe and beyond before drifitng off to sleep. As I settled under the covers, my mind shifted into cuddle time—with a guy who was mediocre at cuddling, but hey, that's my love language so I took what I could get.

He had different ideas about our evening. Big believed with his whole heart that our world was headed for impending doom. He saw floods, no cellular power, or any power at all in our immediate future. He was prepared. He had water, food rations, and CB radios for all of his family members. He grabbed his laptop and headed toward the bed.

Oh no, I thought, here it comes. He showed me photographs of what our little world would look like after the flood. Doom and gloom. I'd prefer a peaceful bedtime story.

I stayed and lovingly turned my attention to Big. He wanted me to make him a promise, and in that he was adamant.

"Promise me that you will have a plan."

That included, but was not limited to, exiting to high grounds, saying goodbye to loved ones, and escaping the state. He looked at my Oregon friend's location and told me that they were doomed and I should point them in a safe direction far in advance. I realized that this was coming from a state of concern and love. This was the best way he could show me that I was on his short list of people that he wanted to see make it through what he thought was Armageddon. This was his form of a love proposal, which was very different from mine.

I told him I would indeed formulate a plan, and that was the ticket to end the lecture.

Yippee, he was up for cuddle time before we drifted off to the slumber his magical bed offered us. The Mayan calendar had reached its end and we were all still here. I was glad. I was sure his CB radios were still charged and his paper maps were handy.

What I had with Big oftentimes bewildered me. What was he thinking in terms of our relationship? We spent just enough time together to keep me invested, but not enough for me to feel wholly or uniquely embraced.

I asked him straight up one time when he seemed so cavalier about me. "Why am I even here?"

His response came quickly and easily; an answer I will never forget.

"Because you don't bug me."

I was speechless. I could only question myself: Why would I justify such a belittling comment? I would love to have a do over and be able to respond that his words "bugged" me. Instead, bitterly confused, I sat in silence.

Was it the opulence that stifled me? I hated to think that was it. I had been around bigger and better. But maybe he was too big for me? How could I see beyond Big and into myself? Maybe he was so big he could not see beyond himself?

Big's master bathroom was perfectly equipped and designed for his and hers. I wondered, did the empty sink designated *"for her"* mock him in his daily regime? Did this powerful man that could achieve so much according to the standards of society feel the emptiness of the unused sink? Did Big have any level of awareness when the absence of mirror splatter from the *"hers"* section of his bathroom palace indicated a missing companion?

Okay, I think I'm getting it! On the *"his"* side of the bathroom, he had plastered on the mirror a one-dollar bill written in red ink to indicate one hundred million dollars. I should have known the moment I saw this. That was Big's vision board! His goals and aspiration were focused on the Big number. Not on skipping hand in hand into the sunset with a five-foot-ten blonde that likes to dance in the kitchen.

My vision board looked very different. One man, four horses, four dogs . . .

Back Into The Shark Tank

"Many people continue to think of sharks as man-eating beasts. Sharks are enormously powerful and wild creatures, but you're more likely to be killed by your kitchen toaster than a shark!"

—Ted Danson

I GAINED STRENGTH KNOWING BIG WAS STILL FISHING ONLINE. IF HE was online, well, then I would be too. I felt stupid sitting and waiting for a guy to come around.

Diving back in, I decided to goose and gander it up. One more time, feet first, into the busy world of online dating. I marketed myself closer to a Super Bowl Sunday advertisement. I had some great photos and saucy writing. If feathers were going to fly, I had plucked the duck. I had two commercials under my belt, after all—I was a paid commercial actress! Step out of the way, dammit, I should be able to add some spice to my profile, and undeniably I did. I had been on for four weeks, and my jazzed-up profile had been viewed over 2,500 times.

Ten percent of the men that checked out my profile sent me some sort of attention, such as likes, winks, and emails. I tried to respond to them all and be up front with the ones who did not fit. To the insistent boy who was twenty, or the "spry" grandfather that was seventy-six, my witty response was, "I do not sense a match here, but I bet Miss Right is right around the corner."

I had to be real with the men I didn't sense *any* connection with. I viewed it as a part-time job, and I aimed to be brave and smart about whom I would allow myself to meet. I always got their last name and met at a public place. I never left the table or my drink alone. I always let someone know where I was and whom I was with.

Also, I kept my standards high and my expectations, well, low. I took it all with a light heart knowing that there may be a reason I met someone. It was always about me and not them. Why did I attract them? If I find myself attracting a huge mess, it only mirrors what I need to look at in myself. The healthier I am, the better off I will be to find and sustain a sweet match.

I knew deep in my heart Big and I were not over. I was the balloon and he felt like the anchor to me. Maybe he wanted another anchor to keep him company?

I would not call or text Big or send a courier pigeon; no smoke signals would drift his way. He'd have to reach out to me, only to find a happy, perky, busy, productive, strong gal on the end of the phone line. Oh, and yes, I would not pick up when he called, and it would take a bit to get back to him. That was the only way to keep his interest. Not by being a whimpering, needy, gushing girl. Instead, I would be a force to be reckoned with and nothing less. My "rules" changed with each man, because each man was different. And yet how different were they really?

EXCEPTION

"I have known exceptional people who have en-
dured severe trials while others, at least on the
surface, seem to have lived charmed lives."
—JOSEPH B. WIRTHLIN

WAITING FOR BIG TO ROLL AROUND MAY HAVE BEEN THE BEST thing that ever happened to me, because I met the most accomplished, interesting man in that lapse of time. Like I said before, when I meet men online, I always get their last name. The very least I do is Google them or search for them on Facebook. They need to be who they say they are, simple as that.

When Exception gave me his last name, I dashed off to quickly Google him. Uh, oh, golly. I was astounded; dozens of websites were dedicated to him. I did not know where to start. His career was diverse. An actor, model, coach, Olympic medalist, professional basketball player, NFL player, and liver transplant survivor. My head was spinning. I freaked out a bit and hit the treadmill, as if going two miles at a trot-walk would help me become instantly in shape for a date two hours away.

Shaking off what I had read about this man, I walked into the restaurant like he was any other dude. I thought to myself, "Stick to your usual routine and rules."

Simple rules helped me navigate the dating world. I always covered myself up, with jeans, a nice top and scarf. I decided long ago never to show any skin on meet and greets. Without rules, I knew I would just lose myself in the midst of serial dating. Ugh, I had become a serial dater.

The instant I met him, I forgot about all the details I gathered on him. Instead, I only wanted to know what was behind his brown eyes that could light up any room. I went straight for the core of the matter and gleaned what was pertinent to me at that moment. I could read about the journey he had been on via the web, but those details lacked where his heart had been.

While sitting across from him at a quaint Asian fusion restaurant, ironically the same place I had my first date with Big, Exception slid both hands along the table, reaching for mine. We sat in silence, holding hands, in a stare off. A magical moment was happening, and I knew it.

He was so beautiful. Someone's mother once said, "Never date anyone prettier than you."—I might have to make an exception. Exception's Mother was Irish and his father Jamaican. He was raised in Canada with three siblings. He had beautiful cinnamon mocha skin and dimples that made me lose my train of thought.

I was from Orange County, and, as a result, the number of black people around my town was low. I could not recall ever meeting a single African-American person while growing up. After we nibbled on a couple of appetizers, we strolled across the street to The Montage. I'm not sure if my feet ever hit the ground. We plopped ourselves down on a sofa to listen to the pianist. Unfortunately, my friend Piano Man had taken the night off. Exception took hold of my hand, dwarfing mine.

It was necessary for me to allow myself to date someone who fell so far out of my normal. He looked at me and began to serenade me. His voice vibrated its way through my body in waves that were capturing my heart. Never do I lack something to say, but this time I was speechless. I sat next to him like a shy schoolgirl with a hopeless crush, gobsmacked, unashamedly gawking at him. The voice in my head scolded me. "Don't stare at him. Stop looking at him." Exception was so pretty, I found myself drowning in a pool of brown eyes and dimples. I was praying he would not notice all that I was thinking. He was off the charts gorgeous and off my dating chart altogether.

My list of dating criteria was matter-of-fact: Long-term relationship man, previously married, grown children (the children and the man), successful, and decent income. Exception did not fit any one of my requirements.

FISHING FOR MEN

"Many men go fishing all of their lives without knowing that it is not fish they are after."
—HENRY DAVID THOREAU

EXCEPTION AND I BEGAN DATING OFF AND ON. WE FORMED A great friendship along the way, figuring out if there was anything romantic between us. We fooled around like a couple of teenagers keeping their clothes on. I was overjoyed at gathering an insight into this intriguing man.

However, five days went by without a word from him, and I knew for a fact that he was checking his online status. Should I give up the online scene? Would I find the same thing with two different guys? Are they all the same, boys in a toy store with too many choices? I had no idea, and I fell fast asleep that night without hearing from Big or Exception.

Thank God for my Egyptian cotton sheets and great girlfriends. I was sorrowfully lacking the attention that lay dormant in the depth of my heart's desire. Should I have lowered my expectations? I say no! I understood what I needed: to be loved for who I am with enough attention to capture my heart.

I had to ask myself an obvious question: Was I choosing the ones who want to play and passing on the ones who want to stay?

Katie L. Lindley

Moreover, did I not feel worthy of sustainable love?

Before getting out my boxing gloves and pummeling myself, I needed to get some beauty sleep. I had a photo shoot in the morning—thank you Star Dresser for the connection. I wished I'd worked out harder. I wished my thighs didn't look like a lunar landing. I wished Exception had called, especially seeing how he said we would see each other that day. I wished I was not feeling so damn sad and lost in a sea of mishaps. Tossed around by my own poor choices. If wishes and buts were candy and nuts, we'd all have a merry Christmas. Whoever said that was a genius.

Knowing I wanted a full night's sleep, I threw back a couple of shots of the devil's liquor, tequila. Not my smartest move.

Soon, I sent a text to Exception, and I was immediately humiliated by it. Tequila text-sleeping bloopers. I knew better. It was midnight and a full moon that night. I'd blame it on that.

He sent a note back. Something to the effect of, "How was your day, baby?"

Right, like that solves everything? By that time, the tequila had gotten to me and I passed out. About an hour into my tequila-coma sleep, he called. As if things were not bad enough, they got worse. I got silly when I answered his call. I said exactly what was on my mind, very dangerous stuff! Something to the effect that I would *not* pursue him (clearly not true), and I would *beg* him for sex (clearly true). It was the booze, the moon, and, well, I wanted *that* man in *my* bed.

DATING CIRCUIT

"I don't have a girlfriend. But I do know a woman who'd be mad at me for saying that."

—MITCH HEDBERG

FINALLY, EXCEPTION AND I GOT AROUND TO SEEING EACH OTHER; maybe it was a date? Or were we "hanging out?" Kissing friends? I had no clue, I've never had a kissing friend before.

Was there a prize in this box of Cracker Jacks? I must not objectify these men as "Jacks," sweet popcorn stuffed into a box, placing myself as the "prize," although I was! I had to take time to see the potential match in each and every guy. That is probably why I was so tired.

I decided to get back into the online game while I waited for Big to figure out if he was going to chase me or not, or where my friendship/ relationship was going with Exception. Exception told me he wanted to date someone half his age plus seven years. How did I fit into that? I was fifty-three and he was fifty-one, no denying with that math, I would never factor into his equation. Why were we dating? Oh, brown eyes, dimples, spectacular kisser, duh.

I took the next night off from dating. Or, we can say I decided to date myself that night. It was just what I needed. A good movie, two glasses of red wine, and a crackling fire. It felt great to hang out by myself.

I was still working on making sure I fit more "me" time into my schedule.

THE HEALER

"She generally gave herself very good advice,
(though she very seldom followed it)."

—LEWIS CARROLL

WITH ALL OF MY LOVE CONFUSION, I DECIDED TO SEE MY FRIEND Healer. Healer and I had been friends for years; we had a soulful and instant connection. She saw me as a client before we became friends. I met her in yoga, where she was teaching meditation. She also was a massage therapist and offered awakening healing. She heals people from any mental, energetic, or physical blocks within the body. She is an intuitive being and guides with the heart of a guru-healing princess. Healer has long, raven black, wavy hair and looks like she was born in Hawaii, with high cheekbones and a smile that lights up a room. She dresses bohemian and possesses a kind gentle spirit. Her eyes fly open at the sound of vulgar talk. She is a true sensitive. I try to lock down my unhinged potty mouth when I am around her.

As our friendship evolved, I began seeing Healer for weekly healing sessions. Healer's work with me was powerful, and the effects of her sessions were noticeable. She seamlessly evolved into my spiritual go-to with great insight and wisdom. She guided me to understand that *I* attracted my own mess. We worked on pulling up old wounds to lay them to rest, cutting the energetic cords I had attached to my past drama and heartache.

We were not all business all the time. We played together as well. Some days, we would be dancing to reggae, drinking mojitos. On other days, we would reflect on great soulful wisdom. She taught a class on intuition that I rarely missed; it was very cool. Who doesn't want to be more intuitive? More than just listening to my gut, I can read things far beyond if my intentions are pure. I simply adore this girl and was blessed that I could always turn to her. She helped heal negative thoughts that consistently caused blocks within all aspects of my life. I too became a sounding board she could go to, and that made our circle complete.

I recognized that my covert behavior was attracting unavailable men. I wanted to clear this from my energy DNA. The dating patterns that I created were driving me bonkers. Healer and I went right to the heart of the matter on a Friday afternoon, looking at what my behavior and choices had been and where they came from. I could feel the rapid results as my heart started to shift about my familiar dating rituals.

Why was I waiting for Big? What was I doing with Exception? I needed to reflect on my choices. Healer did some healing work on me on that particularly confusing Friday. She told me to be thankful for all that I *did* have around me at the time. Going through the gratitude process always shifted my thinking. I woke up that Saturday morning, knowing I had to hide my profile from online viewing.

During this healing time, I decided to give myself a break from Big and all men. Healer helped me see that I was extremely grateful for my loving circle of girlfriends. I was blessed to call Healer one of my dearest of friends. She was a bright light that came into this world to share her love and healing, awakening souls to live out their life's purpose. Knowing her had changed my life. She was simply without judgment of others and lovingly laughed at all my current antics. I was working at cherishing my female friendships. She had spirit-filled wisdom and insight into the past and future.

Who wouldn't want that in a friend?

THE BACHELORETTE, OR
BACK TO SQUARE ONE

"There's only two people in your life you should
lie to . . . the police and your girlfriend."
—JACK NICHOLSON

HAPPY THAT I HAD GIVEN MYSELF A COUPLE OF MONTHS OFF from online dating, gaining renewed strength from precious time with Healer, I was willing to let myself be "out there" in the dating world, vulnerable but safe. I felt much like The Bachelorette, minus the stylist, makeup artist, and world-class locations. So, nothing at all like The Bachelorette.

I was sorting through men, and they were all pretty great in their own way. How did they fit with me and what did I want? I was growing weary and found myself tired of the same scene. I was diligently listening to online seminars on soul mate love and pouring through all my dating books that had been gathering dust. I was gaining knowledge and insight, especially into myself, but I felt cranky and unrested—like a toddler needing a nap. This Bachelorette was ready to take a long commercial break.

Is it basic human nature to desire what we don't have in a relationship? Those who are married want the freedom that singlehood brings. Those who are single want the closeness and continuity of a relationship. Why is it that everyone wants what everyone else seems to have? Begs the question, is the grass really greener on the other side of the fence? Based upon that thought, perhaps I'll dye my pubic hair green—it can't hurt.

New Year Rolled Around

"Cheers to a new year and another chance for us
to get it right."

—Oprah Winfrey

WITH MY BOLD NEW ATTITUDE OF NOT PINING FOR ANY MAN THAT was not interested in spending New Year's Eve with me, I decided to spend new year's alone. This particular new year felt like a significant birthday. It was a moment in time when I needed to question myself and the path I had chosen. I had to find a new lesson and a new understanding in the new year.

This alone time nudged me closer to embracing myself, pushing me further away from caring about Exception or Big. What good was a love if it was lopsided? The answer was absolutely no good at all.

Big, who was off skiing with his kids is in Aspen, did remember to send me a "Happy New Year" text. Exception texted me the next day, whoop whoop.

Perhaps in letting go of men, or the man-boys, I would find myself, and in that, a real love would emerge? Was my love journey meant to be this painful? The idea was to learn about men, but I was slowly discovering I had a lot to learn about myself.

It was time I opened my arms and heart for a real love. Well, I also really wanted to get laid. Two half-men . . . equaled zero sex.

On that quiet New Year's morning, as I soaked in the tiled safe place I called my bathtub, I mustered up all the spirit I could manage and asked for a lover. Alone, in need of the physical touch, I pleaded with God, "*Send me a lover.*" It became my mantra.

I only had to wait two days to get what I asked for, or so I thought.

Get Big Then Get Out . . .

"Attitude is a little thing that makes a big difference."

—Winston Churchill

M Y GIRLFRIEND HEALER WARNED ME, "BE CAREFUL WHAT YOU wish for."

Truer words had never been spoken. Two days after my *"send me a lover"* mantra, I received a call from Big. It had been a couple of months since I had seen him. He was all about business and blah, blah, blah. Droning on and on about himself, his dreams, and his life. It seemed great to be caught up on his life and hear his voice. He told me his stomach was bothering him, and I shared something I had learned from Exception to get his health in order. Exception was an expert in health.

Later that day, I drove up to Big's to drop off some Slippery Elm Bark. This magical cure was to help his stomach ailments. It was great to see him; he looked good—Aspen must have done wonders for him. I walked in strutting my stuff and made myself at home on his lap. Big was sitting at his kitchen counter, and we were affectionately sharing a bar stool. I was quickly taken aback by our familiar kisses. Within moments, we found ourselves in the throes of passion. He scooped me off my feet and carried me into his office, tearing the place up like a scene from a movie, items were flying off his hundred-year-old desk. I found myself upside down staring at the oak crown molding and hand painted ceiling, with paper clips stuck in my hair. I was clearly bewildered; after all, I had asked for a *"lover."* Was this what *I* wanted? There was such power in my request.

Was I the one he wanted just for sex? Was that *his* purpose for me? Wasn't this what *I* wanted? Was that my agenda? Then again, it was my personal *"send me a lover"* mantra. I did help myself to his lap. We had crazy tear-your-clothes-off lovemaking session, but my spirit was confused. Our brief heated moment was evident all over his office: papers flying, a stapler landed God knows where, and where were all the Post-it notes?

Post-it notes, *yes*, they could help me. I needed to make a Post-it note to myself: *STOP*!!!!!

If I could have found the damn Post-it notes, I would have done just that.

Instead, we headed up to his master bathroom.

There was a comfort level between us that felt reassuring. We chatted like old friends. I plopped myself down on the granite vanity on the "her" side of the bathroom while he was showering. Big's bathroom had an open design. We held eye contact as the multitude of shower-heads hit his body, as he washed himself of me. It felt altogether familiar. I was still off-kilter. I was feeling wonky, as my head was spinning. I was not sure why I was feeling that way. Was this vertigo . . . post-coital-vertigo? I may have just invented a post-sexual disorder. What do I get for that? Maybe a Post-it-note stuck to my head.

Big ushered me out to my car, and, like the polite son of a preacher man does, he then gave me a simple kiss goodbye. I watched him close his big front door and allowed myself a moment while sitting in my car in front of his home. I came to help him and he helped himself to me. I realized I had to listen to what my heart wanted. Sadness came over me and I finally said, *"I want more!"* out loud, for no one to hear but myself. I heard my own voice as I spoke these words. With those words hanging in the air, I exited Big's neighborhood.

I drove the Coast Highway home and had an uneasy feeling the entire way. I wanted a *"lover,"* so why was I so conflicted? My gut knew the answer before I did.

I prayed: *"Oh Dear Lord, here I am. It's me, and okay, I messed up, let's chat."* The ride down the Coast Highway was quiet, yet loud. I drove in silence with my thoughts and a real need for a hot salt bath.

The morning, before our tryst, Big told me he had been off the online dating scene for a couple of months. I checked when I got home, and he was actively online within one hour of my departure. Did he think I was stupid? Did he think this was the only way he could get me? By lying? His manhood was still swimming around in my lady business! I was faced with yet another dilemma with him. I knew from past experience not to show my hand or react too quickly. This time my pie hole stayed shut; it was glued with self-loathing. That was not a great taste in my mouth.

I decided I would wait until the date he promised me the following week. I would approach him as a babe in control of herself. I planned to share with him how trust factored into my world. I would ask him directly, at just the right moment, why he had lied to me about the dating site. The only way I would have any kind of relationship with someone, anyone, was with honesty. I now knew that lesson in spades. I cared about Big; I hoped he cared enough about me to come clean. I did want a lover, but within several hours of getting what I asked for, the request felt so complicated and vacant. Healer's words were dancing a jig in my head. I think they were wearing wooden clogs.

"Be careful what you ask for!" *Ugh.*

I really wanted Big to be more than what he was. I saw an end game with him. We had painted the same picture of our futures. He participated in this shared illusion and had his hand in it. I had to step back. I had no choice, as his vision of us differed from mine. Big was who he was long before I got there.

Was Big a big disappointment, or were my expectations skewed? I would have preferred to put most of the blame on myself, hence a better path for learning and self-discovery. I thought, "Oh Lord. Isn't this what it was truly all about, understanding *myself?*"

Big had many grandiose ideas. Pushing sixty, he was setting out to accomplish different projects that a mere mortal man could only look up to. Had I done the proper calculations? A girlfriend or wife were not in his cards. His view of himself was high and mighty. His view of me was not flattering. He saw me as wild and flighty. Of course, he wanted to ride that filly, just not introduce her to his business partners or bring her home to meet his parents.

Just A Little Too Much Of Big

"Trust your gut. You know yourself, so don't let somebody else tell you who you are."

—Tatiana Maslany

A couple of months later, after our passionate moment in his office, I had dinner with Big and his son. That proved to be interesting. His son was charming and engaging, and our energies flowed at the same level. Big was more of the observer, yet he'd chime in now and again while his son and I easily kept the conversation going.

Big's son said to me during the course of the evening, "So where do you see yourself in ten years?"

I proceeded to describe a life with horses, dogs, snow, yoga, and organic farming.

From a pure heart that loved his father, he stated, "That is exactly what my Dad wants. Why don't you two just get *over* yourselves and move on and have your life together?"

Big and I may have scooted an inch or two away from one another. Honest words were firing, and we did not want to catch a bullet from the fallout.

It is not easy to be called out on your "deal," especially from your adult child.

We had a lovely evening. I thoroughly enjoyed these handsome men. Big told me he wanted to chat alone with me because something was on his mind. When we arrived at Big's home, we made our way to his bedroom and sat in the two chairs that cornered the fireplace.

I made myself comfortable and sat cross-legged in the oversized chair that faced Big's matching chair. I didn't see this conversation coming at all. He proceeded to tell me what was wrong with me. Yes, he sat me down for a PowerPoint presentation of my faults.

What?

This was his list:

1. You falsely portray yourself as having a great deal of knowledge spanning many interesting subjects.
2. Your facts pertaining to any specific subject are just enough to get by and fake it.
3. You only truly know ten percent of any subject you ever start talking about.
4. You are assuming the role as my significant other.

I mean, he even gave an estimated calculation of ten percent. Big summed up the whole idea of me into a math equation. He said I only knew ten percent of anything I ever talked about. After the brutality of these kindly delivered insults, he then carefully worded and stated that I posture myself as his girlfriend. It was as if I was auditioning for the leading role of "Mrs. Big." Continuing to evaluate me, he said that I was all over the map and not capable of being great at any one thing. He said all of these things as politely as he would have offered someone sweet tea during a sunny summer afternoon while seated on a white porch in the South.

This painful conversation dragged on for nearly an hour. Why did I sit there and take his damning and critical view of me? He had me cornered like a dumb animal. Or rather, I allowed him to corner me.

What was even worse—I used sex to make it stop! I did! I found a way to get him to stop talking. Did I really do that? Oh Lord, I did . . .

I slipped out of my chair. In a cat-like fashion, I crawled over to him and prostrated myself at his feet. I was just thinking: make it stop! Where were the Post-it notes when I needed them? I couldn't bear to hear one more word about how utterly inadequate I was as a human being. How I presented myself as a lie, just "making it up" as I went along to get by. And how I wanted to assume the position as "Mrs. Big." With my hands on his knees, gazing up into his eyes, suddenly and gratefully, his words got lost. He put his hands on my shoulders and brushed my hair back from my face. I am certain he viewed me as a wounded bird. This was easy; maybe I wasn't as dumb as he thought. Look who just lost his damning words. It was wrong to have sex with this man, but I felt strangely empowered. I am sure he felt as though he was literally driving his point home.

Did he take advantage of me? Did I take advantage of him? He was in love with his manhood and rightly should have been, as that part of him was, um, well, he was Big. Honestly, he wasn't for me. He never took time to see to my needs. I never took the time or had the courage to teach him about my needs. His needs, his time, his agenda, that seemed to be the deal between us.

I was not sure if I agreed with his carefully presented data of me. His version of me was very misconstrued. I became painfully aware that what he thought about me was not flattering. Or, what he knew about me made me feel bad and uncertain. I pondered, was he close to the truth or far away? He may have had some merit after all. Perhaps I don't take critique very well?

We did what we did, and I left with steaming hostility towards myself. Why did I have passionate sex with a man who did not even come close to respecting me? Why should this man respect me when clearly, my choices, behavior, and self-admission illustrated I was not respecting myself? Leaving his home when he started to put me down ever so politely would have shown us both an ounce of dignity. Instead, I *reinforced* what he believed about me in spades.

Hurrying into my waiting leather seats, I drove away as fast as my fancy car could go, as self-revulsion followed me. It sat next to me like a passenger riding shotgun. I was surprised that the seat belt bell wasn't chiming, or was it? Self-revulsion can be heavy, and it was ringing incessantly in my head.

The four and four drove deep into my soul. Four horses, four dogs, white picket fence, organic gardening. That was what I truly wanted. This Midwestern son of a preacher man that thinks outside of the box dumbfounded me. It was time to let go of that fantasy.

It was far too easy to shut down with Big. Phone calls were simply absent, without caring from either party. It was kind of sad, but it was time. We just became sparse and polite. I was done with regrets. I could do better, and I knew it. The healing effects of Healer began taking place and I knew that as well.

Thank you Big, for showing me exactly what you thought of me. Thank you, Healer, for showing me no man can ever fix me and that I am not broken.

I Took A Lover

"A lover without indiscretion is no lover at all."
—Thomas Hardy

A TRUE LADY NEVER REVEALS HER DRESSMAKER OR HER LOVER. "Here I go," I thought, "This was it, it just had to be." Perhaps my desire for love skewed reality, leaving me with the immediate mistakable choice of accepting the consolation prize. Then again, I could recall that my request for a "lover" was not made too long ago. The man behind door number two looked really, very good.

Lover was a year younger than me, fifty-three, as I had just turned fifty-four. Lover came in a six-foot-two package, with thick and unruly peppery hair he slicked back into a frozen hold with a gob of hair goo. His eyes had a way of changing colors with his mood or environment. I had a mood ring in fifth grade I stared at for hours. It was later replaced by Lover's eyes. I would say they were hazel, but I had seen them turn light brown and grey on colder days. His daily outfit consisted of an old flannel shirt, cargo shorts, black socks, and old Adidas sneakers.

Lover and I matched up in so many ways. We met at a coffee shop, and I swooned at the sight of him. Our pre-meeting phone conversation had been so flat that I just threw on jeans, a sweater, and UGG boots. I wasn't too excited about meeting this one.

He sat in the corner with his chair and body facing away from me.

I squared off and faced him, giving him my full attention. I should have known then that body language does not lie. After what I perceived to be a great conversation, we walked to his car to meet his six dogs and one foster dog. He had a Mercedes van rigged up to suit his canine family. I stood there and loved on his dogs; they were a mishmash of beloved rejected mutts.

I asked, "So, you're going to call me, right?"

He looked at me and said, "I didn't think you liked me."

I playfully pushed his beautiful chest and refuted. In that moment, it was necessary to muster up my best flirt action and make my intentions known. I liked him.

Thankfully, Lover did call to set up our second date. He decided that we would take the dogs for a hike and then go out for lunch. I knew I just wanted to spend time with him. I had that feeling of wanting to crawl into his shirt pocket and stay there for the next ten years or so. He was smart, handsome, kind, and a caregiver. I am a sucker for the caregivers.

Our hike was charming, as we trekked the back hills of Rancho Santa Fe. The dogs had a swim in a small pond to cool off from the hot dry weather. That swim caused the van ride home to be filled with a thick, swampy dog smell. Somehow, all I could smell was the sweetness of our date.

After our hike, we headed to the quaint nearby village for lunch. Lover thoughtfully parked his custom kennel-on-chrome-wheels and left it running with the doors unlocked and air conditioning on. I liked the way this guy rolled. He felt life was on his side and that he was safe. No wonder I wanted to crawl into his pocket. Why wouldn't I?

One great date rolled into the next, and I got excited about the thought of him and the thought of us. We held hands, hugged, and seemed to fit rather well together.

Everything was going smoothly, except for that one minor detail. What was that? Do I have to brace myself once again? Much to my frustration, he had never kissed me. I began to question myself and my desirability. Lover was the quiet type; his slight awkwardness was adorable. Our conversations did not roll on for hours as he was a man of few words.

We had a lunch date lined up for the next day. That same night I got a dreadful text. Yes, a text, which shows he might not be an actual stand-up kind of a guy. He was a man standing in the shadows of his own decision.

Lover stated that he did not sense "relationship chemistry" between us and asked if we could be friends.

Doubling over in hurt and disappointment, I texted back, "I have enough male friends. No thank you."

We texted back and forth as sorrow settled into my bones. I should have been angry that this was all taking place via text. I wasn't. I understood on some level that his way of communicating was not ordinary. Lover laid somewhere between odd and extraordinary.

The next morning, I sent him a text message thanking him for being forthright with me and wishing him the best. It was something to the effect of, "Let me know how your life goes. Hugs."

He reached out to me via text a couple of hours later and suggested we become lovers and friends. I felt pissed. That was what he wanted me to be? How is it that I wanted more and was contemplating less? Why did he think we would be great at being lovers? After all, we had never even kissed! I had to wonder, why not a real relationship? I was so confused. Had I become the girl who is so willing to compromise in relationships that she ends up with the scraps?

The heart wants what the heart wants, and mine told me loud and clear I wanted this man in my life. With the volume turned up, my head told me that I did not want to not know him. A double negative—that should have given me a clue. I agreed to meet him so we could talk. I wanted to understand exactly what he had in mind.

I drove onto the familiar street at his address. Even the curb was expensive, maintained, and waiting for me. I felt nervous as I approached his beautiful home. Like a girl walking into a babysitting interview, I suddenly felt small, excited, and less than empowered.

Corona Del Mar is like a gold coin sitting in the pocket of Newport Beach. It is shiny within the castle walls but hidden from most people's eyes. Lover's home sat over the water in an exclusive neighborhood called Irvine Terrace. Perfectly placed, you could watch sailboats, motorboats, paddle-boards, and seals pass through the harbor. Behind the water sat a peninsula lined with homes two blocks deep, and beyond that was the Pacific Ocean. It was ideal and calm, with the beauty of the finest resort.

Lover made a gorgeous salad with vegetables from his organic garden, barbecued some steak, and popped open a bottle of white wine. Still waiting for our first kiss, we discussed what a *"lover"* relationship would look like. It sounded much like a girlfriend without the girlfriend part. Travel and extended weekends were included. Sexual monogamy, his idea, go figure, was noted as important and mutually agreed upon. Honesty was also stated as a requirement. This was all penciling out, but where was the notary?

He was doing most of the talking. Suddenly, he was a man of many words.

Wasn't that my mantra? I wanted a lover, damn it!

It was: "Be careful what you wish for . . ." Healer's words returned to me uninvited. I pushed away the fear and listened to my heart—or was it my vagina? They can both be very loud.

On the other side of this arrangement, the dark side, he would be dating and seeking out other women. With that fact known, so would I. Once either one of us found the "one," our "deal" would be "off." Was I clearly setting myself up for the ultimate esteem crusher?

I knew damn good and well that no other man would ever stand a fighting chance with me. My noisy heart and vagina seemed to be linked like Siamese twins. Lover was offering everything to me on a fancy silver platter with a bay view, except what I truly wanted. It was so close but so far away. I wanted a man to be crazy for me, adore me, and only me. I wanted to be crazy for one guy and build on that. Isn't that how it's done? Why did I once again choose a man that did not *really* want me?

Feeling the effects of this man, the proximity of our bodies, combined with the salt air, white wine, and the lovely meal, it all intoxicated me into a gooey love gob. I paused for a moment while he waited for an answer from me. "*No*" and I were a thousand miles apart, "*yes*" and I were feeling great, sharing the couch with Lover.

I agreed to our arrangement; of course I did. I then suggested that we kiss. I mean, after all, it is a very important factor. I flipped myself around like a skilled circus act, allowing him to realize just how lucky he was. I playfully landed on his lap. The kiss was better than fine. Fine would not even be in the description. Maybe I was the one who just got lucky?

Lover was very talented as a lover, go figure. He was a giver: he was patient, and his endowment and bank account perhaps rivaled for the largest. It was overwhelming. His kisses alone were enough to put me under a spell. He became a drug I had to have. He would pleasure me with the heart of a warrior, never leaving the battlefield until the mission was accomplished. I found myself lost, melting as he had his way with me. He took all the time that was required while going down on me.

I was thrilled with my Lover. Our sweet times together were blissful. We formulated a routine that was easy. I was completing my two-hundred-hour yoga teacher training, so he oftentimes had to wait for me to show up, all tuckered out and freakishly limber after many hours of yoga class.

I was sitting on Lover's granite kitchen counter after a long yoga day, sipping on white wine. The sun had peacefully set behind the bay into the Pacific Ocean, as a few boats were still trailing into their appointed docks. I oftentimes found myself in this same spot on Lover's kitchen counter as he worked his way around the kitchen. I love a man that can cook!

I innocently asked, as politely as I could muster, "Has any girl ever tapped out due to your size?" This question had been with me for quite a while.

He readily answered, "No."

I began wondering if his highly skilled oral talents were developed in order to get the girl ready, willing and able to handle his endowment package.

During one of our post-coital conversations, I inquired, "Why are you so good at that?"

He said, "It's not that hard to figure out."

I was thinking that some things came easy for Lover. Making money, making love, he's got that all down just right.

My past experiences left me feeling anxious over lovemaking. I felt like a race was ahead of me and I had to hurry up to meet my partner at the finish line like a sprinter. The sense of competition was in the air, but experiencing performance anxiety sadly was my norm. Not so with Lover; we had nothing but time. He left me longing for more, and I chased after Lover for my next fix. Huge mistake.

I never quite got a handle on Lover's success. He out-banked anyone I had ever known (at that point) by an astounding margin. His home in Austin, Texas was for sale for 11.5 million dollars. He said that the appraisers had a hard time with anything priced over ten million.

I nodded, and eked out a, "Oh, uh-huh."

That was not what I liked about him; it just was a part of who he was. We always did simple things together that required little to no money. Throughout the course of our time together, the house sold for what he was asking. We popped open a bottle of Cristal. Bubbly fun.

Well into our lover arrangement, I struck up a futile conversation. "It's not about money, it's about the connection you have with each other. That is what matters," I said, feebly trying to convince him.

Waving at his lavish surroundings, he retorted, "Yeah, but it's a helluva a lot better with all this!"

"Money can make all your choices different and better, health included," he added.

He was right.

Instead of arguing a moot point, I stripped to nudity and slipped into his private outdoor Jacuzzi connected to his master bath. Laying my head on the cement, my hair strewn out behind me like a mermaid, my body drifted across the bubbling water. I gazed up at the night sky through the palm trees. Lover readily joined me with a bottle of champagne and two crystal champagne flutes as we relaxed and chatted. Ah, I thought. Champagne, the gateway drug to romance. His Jacuzzi seemed to be the place where we bared our souls and talked for hours on end. Naked Lover is a chatter. He was more than just a lover; he was a friend. The truth be told under the stars, until we pruned up and were forced to exit.

Lover mentioned going away with the dogs on a two-month road trip. I was game. His fear was that we would become too close, and it would be too romantic, leading one of us to getting hurt. (Too late for that! How was champagne and sitting under the stars in a Jacuzzi not romantic?) He hemmed, hawed, fussed, and squirmed. I loved the idea; it sounded like so much fun! Dogs, Lover, and the roads that lay ahead? I'm in! I tried to proclaim my formidable independence. The strong woman I am can handle the closeness this trip would bring. I would not fall in love. I said I would *not*—further lying to myself. Much to my dismay, the trip never happened.

On another Jacuzzi night, while we were discussing being lovers, he said, "No one is impervious to hurt when you open yourself up for real lovemaking." With tears in his eyes, he added, "Real love is letting someone go toward the love that they are seeking and deserving of." It sounded like a crock of crap, but with our "deal," the possibility of me leaving him was in the back of his mind (if he only knew). At that very moment, I sadly understood he was preparing to let me go. I just didn't know when that time would be. I neatly pushed those thoughts away.

I was ready for a man who wanted me in more ways and dimensions than he did. He was still figuring himself out. Or maybe he never really saw me as being worthy of anything other than being his lover? However one spins this, I was fated for a lonely road ahead. That was the road I decided to travel on. I put myself in this relationship, I had a choice and I landed here.

I should have known the single man with the seven dogs held the same reputation as the single woman with six cats. The dogs were everywhere all the time. They must have understood Daddy's ways as they peacefully ignored our boisterous lovemaking. Yes, they slept with us, or at least several of the small ones did. It is one thing to politely gag down a forgotten pubic hair that did not find the right end of a razor (thank God for the glass of water next to the bed), but it's quite another altogether to be swallowing down dog hairs. I grew attached to those little canine beasts.

Lover had baby talk with them. I know. Yuck, right? Baby talk words made their way to me, but the dogs got the lot of his affection. I easily talked to the dogs the same way. If I thought he was a big weirdo, then so was I.

The unwelcoming text came to me on a Thursday. Lover said that he had met someone and wanted to be true to this new girl. Our original agreement was that we would be forthright about wanting to change course if one of us found that special someone to have it "all" with. I signed up for the "lover package" and settled. My heart hit the floor when I read this; I couldn't breathe.

My first reaction was, "I am so happy for you!"

That was one thing I found solace in; my reaction to him was positive. My second reaction seemed as if I was a bit more invested than I cared to admit to him. I had started to fall in love with my Lover. What a terrible blunder.

Mad Skills . . .
My Dear Friend Healer

> "Good night, good night! Parting is such sweet sorrow, that I shall say goodnight till it be morrow."
>
> —William Shakespeare, *Romeo and Juliet*

THE VERY NEXT NIGHT I WENT OUT WITH ONE OF MY BEST GIRL-friends, Healer. She is bright, loving, and fun. I needed some fun. We sat outside the Ritz Carlton in Dana Point, overlooking the beautiful Pacific. It was a balmy night. As the sun slowly sank into the magical sea, everyone was happy. We had strangers buying us drinks as they quickly became our new friends. A curly-haired guitar player arrived on the scene to make it ever more surreal. He looked like he had jumped off his surfboard after whipping by Disney studios for a brief photo shoot. I guessed his name was "Chad." It just had to be.

Understanding my recent heartache, Healer sat by my side and encouraged me to be in the moment. We turned outside of my problems and had fun with the new people we were meeting. It seemed to be just what I needed.

We enjoyed every moment as we made our way through evening margaritas, appetizers, and songs. Tables of people came and went, like the tide below us. We happily stayed as witnesses to the picture-perfect night.

Healer was bolstering me, telling me I had "mad skills."

She noted how our drinks were getting paid for with a smile and a giggle. These so-called "mad skills" could get me just about anything I wanted in life. However, with the recent sting of rejection, her affirming words did not resonate with me. I knew her heart for me was true; that I could feel. We were gratefully placed in a special moment, watching the dusk settle over us, as the moon did its job illuminating the Pacific Ocean. It was nothing short of breathtaking. Everyone sitting on the beautiful outdoor patio deck had some sort of positive reaction to the perfect evening.

It was getting late, and it was clear that we were closing the place down. As we headed to the valet, I suddenly snapped. I started to cry, and it came out of me like uncontrollable vomit from food poisoning, no filter. It felt as if it came out of nowhere, but the longer it went on, the more it felt like something had been filling me, drowning me, diving deep within me from head to toe.

Healer quickly ducked me into the well-appointed ladies' lounge. We sat on a ridiculously expensive couch, and I found my head on her shoulder as I sobbed. Full-blown, flat-out crying was followed by guttural sounds, and my nose was impolitely running. Healer held me in her arms like a baby as she rubbed my back, rocking me gently.

Tequila shined light on the truth. Where's the warning label on that? Hadn't the surgeon general copped hip to that one late night with his own tequila confessions? It was that scene from a movie where the girl keeps on getting caught up in heartache. My mother would have not approved of this public display of emotion.

Even though I did not believe I was that invested in Lover, my broken heart told me otherwise. Denial was a powerful force that I have had to reconcile with on more than one occasion. This was one of those occasions. I was grateful that this moment brought to the surface what I truly needed. It was okay to feel sorrow. I felt rejected and set aside. It seemed Lover was never that into me. It was time I became into myself; one of us had to. I had visited this town of pain before, and I was ready to kick the dust off my boots and get the heck out of Dodge. Also known as the ladies lounge at the Ritz Carlton.

I must have some sort of mad skills as I became completely unraveled in the arms of a trained professional, my friend Healer. I had an out-of-body experience, realizing that I was in a world of pain, with tequila and sorrow pulsing through my body.

I didn't want to be this girl! Hadn't I already gone through the tough lessons? Why was I here once again? Healer gracefully gave me all the time I needed to release what was trapped inside of me. Everything was a blur of unashamedly bawling, but, eventually, I was ready to suck it up and sulk toward the valet. Not being able to see past my own anguish, Healer put her arm around me, gently guiding, as we walked through the lavish lobby. She drove me home and I realized how blessed I was to have a friend like her, a true angel.

WHAT? MORE LOVER

"A friend is always good to have, but a lover's kiss
is better than angels raining down on me."

—DAVE MATTHEWS

I HONESTLY THOUGHT THAT WAS GOING TO BE THE LAST CHAPTER ON
Lover, hence all the agony that submerged from my body on that fateful
night with Healer. Losing someone applies to friendship as well. I did not
want to know that loss. He was a man I did not want to not know. Once
again, with the double negatives.

A few weeks after the infamous sob scene, I sent Lover a text and told
him I was sad, stressed, and could use a healing hike with him and the
pups. After all, we were friends and I needed a friend. He readily agreed,
and I found myself heading back to his house so we could take the dogs to
the beach.

It was nice to see him, and I was glad I had a friend in him. Lover suggested lunch first, so we sat outside overlooking the bay as boats headed out
to take on this glorious day. It was such a peaceful place, watching people
lulling through the bay.

The oven heated up our pizza as we sipped on white wine. I faced my
chair away from him and turned my head from the conversation. I was
"turning" away from him. One of the small pups was in my lap; it was
Gimpy. His chair was facing me. Lover was turning "toward" me. He told

me things were a disappointment with his new girl. I let it slide. It was none of my business, and I did not care to know. I heard the buzzer go off on one of his dryers.

He said, "Hey, dear, would you help me make my bed?"

"Uh, sure," I replied.

He had a housekeeper five days a week, but, apparently, one of the pups had gotten sick on his sheets.

I dutifully follow him with the fresh sheets into his room. We efficiently made the bed, and he made his move. I was walking out to sit back on the terrace, and he grabbed my arm to turn me toward him. Like a choreographed dance move, I landed square in front of him. He drew me in close and kissed me. I stepped back, spinning on my heels, and bolted outside to my awaiting "facing-away" chair. He followed me and sat down.

Incredulous, I said, "*What was that!?*"

I thought we had shifted into friendship. Lover reminded me about the last time we had made love, and he said it had been too long. He reminded me of details that showed he was paying attention, and that I mattered. Was he wooing me? My heart sank; it sounded like our time had been significant to him as well.

I followed him into the bedroom once more, glad the sheets were clean. The lovemaking was always, every time, great with Lover. The recent rejection he served me was still with me. Sweet served with a side of sour.

Was I in love with the thought of him, or the idea of us? Probably both. Would I be with Lover if I had the option? I would, but I did not have that option. What I wanted was not on the menu. The question was why? Lover never really loved me, yet I still wanted to break through his walls, but then what? End up with a person that had to be convinced that I was fabulous? Was I just a silly human, wanting what I could not have? Thinking I could change someone proved to be extremely disappointing.

Lover was such an endearing, somewhat quirky man. One that, in the long run, could not sustain a real or lasting relationship with me. At least not the kind of relationship I was looking for.

When I look back at some of the guys I was involved with, "asshole" can readily slip from my lips. Well, Lover was not an asshole. What is the opposite of asshole? Lover was one of the good guys, decent, at least with me, in every sense of the word. That might not be fair, because we never dealt with any of the tough stuff. Our connection was all champagne, bubbling Jacuzzis, and starlit skies.

We had a blast on the balance beam. We just never nailed the landing.

What Was Lover Thinking?

"You want a friend in Washington? Get a dog."
—Harry S. Truman

A COUPLE OF WEEKS LATER, I RECEIVED A TEXT FROM LOVER. He suggested I meet his friend that had just moved from the East Coast. Lover told me they had known one another for twenty-five years. I felt flattered at first, although, to be honest with myself, I was still getting over Lover. Cherishing our friendship, I agreed, and Lover gave his friend, East Coast, my number.

East Coast called, and we started chatting, getting to know one another. He said that his home out here was temporary for the next couple of months. He told me that Lover was moving to Oregon with his Buddhist girlfriend.

Oregon, really? Where we talked about going? The place that held my heart was now going to house my ex-Lover, his dogs, and Buddhist girlfriend to boot? Nice. My heart sank quickly, and I stopped breathing. It was official, spoken out loud, Lover had a new girlfriend. This should have not shocked me. Lucky bitch. I didn't hate her, I swear.

Then East Coast told me he was staying at Lover's home. Excuse me, *what?*

Was I supposed to go visit him at the crime scene? The home where we made beautiful music together? Was I just going to wander down the hall to the guest bedroom, even though I knew the minute details of the master suite? Where I would go into Lover's closet to grab a pair of his plaid boxers, white socks, and a T-shirt, mirroring his sleep outfit? We could have posed for our annual Christmas cards in his sleeping attire, but, oh wait, he now had a girlfriend. I'd have to make sure they had my address to receive their Christmas card, or maybe not. She was Buddhist after all.

Did Lover think we could all hang out together? With me knowing his body and his home with such great familiarity? With the dogs following me into the other room? Dogs will give you away every time. Forget that, he's taking the dogs to Oregon. Without a doubt, there was trace evidence of me in the master bathroom. Was I now to leave my DNA on the other side of the house?

I was not mature enough to handle this, nor did I care to be. Dear Lord, would someone please analyze this and get back to me? I did not know what to make of Lover's offer. Could he really be that insensitive?

East Coast and I never stood a chance. I was puzzled with Lover's idea of meeting his friend and realized, on some sweet confused level, he was trying to place me in his life somehow. I knew I would eventually move past my disappointment with Lover.

Accepting that I was worthy of love, acknowledging the rejection I had experienced, and realizing the gift that this relationship had brought me helped me find gratitude even in the disappointment. I became grateful for this bizarre miss-matchmaking, because, in my brief conversation with his friend it all became painfully clear, Lover had moved on and was moving out.

I waited a couple of weeks before I texted East Coast that I had met someone and wanted to see where it could go. This was a classic cowardly way of squirming out of a situation. I did suggest that we still meet for lunch in a couple of weeks. I mean, he was new to town and friends with Lover. He readily agreed. I needed time, and I bought myself some. I would not go back to Lover's house, no way.

SOME YOU THROW
BACK IN THE WATER

"Were I to put myself on . . . one of those online dating things, I would not include in my profile that I'm regularly hospitalized for psychosis. But I do know that when I get really bad, there is a place for me to go where I will feel better."
—MARYA HORNBACHER

MOST OF MY ONLINE DATES, OR MANY OF MY FIRST DATES RATHer, were inconsequential on my journey. Not even worthy of repeating to friends or writing about. They were mostly wonderful guys that were just not the right fit for me. Like trying on shoes, some you don't want to take home, and others you wear out of the store.

I have, however, had a doozy or two that would be fun to share. I mean, really, this stuff happens! I shake my head, a shudder goes through my head to my feet, and not in a good way.

Do I dare mention one of my first dates from the online dating world? I was sitting across from an otherwise fine man. It must have been too much for his nerves, because he was pulling his ear hairs out with his fingers. Then he would rub his hand together, as his wiry unwanted ear hair drifted to the ground. Meanwhile, I took the high road and pretended like it wasn't really happening, but clearly feeling nauseated. Ear Hair Man and I never had a second date. Now to share a couple more examples of some really weird online meeting moments . . .

Ferrari Man

"Here comes 40. I'm feeling my age and I've ordered the Ferrari. I'm going to get the whole mid-life crisis package."

—Keanu Reeves

I MET FERRARI MAN ONLINE. HE LIVED CLOSE TO ME, SO WE AGREED to meet in person. He actually referred to himself as Ferrari Man. He was a highly successful man that worked closely with top athletes and owned several companies.

Ferrari Man was ready to talk about himself at any given time. I met him in a retail parking lot near my home. He stood almost six foot four, was tan, with a thick head of hair, and teeth so white they blinded. You could smell his cologne from fifty paces away. He wore expensive Italian burgundy shoes with a jazzed up, embroidered, white button-down shirt. Why is it that most men have this same shirt in different versions? I paused at the jeans and decided to say it like it was. They were expensive designer pants that were faded, ripped, with his thick tanned hairy legs poking through (like an overgrown picket fence): it was gross.

He approached me, all alpha male, and hugged me to the point of discomfort, not letting me go. I saw this as a power play and told him to release me at once. He found this funny, and I told him to go home

Katie L. Lindley

and put on a decent pair of pants. I would not be manhandled by anyone—who did this guy think he was? We started off on the wrong shoe,
the Italian leather burgundy type nonetheless.

I then agreed to get into his Ferrari to drive a very short distance to
a restaurant I was familiar with. One stoplight away, my hand was on the
door handle. We pulled up as Carlos, the valet, greeted me by name and
kissed me on the check. This threw Ferrari Man for a loop.

He tried to take his power back. "I know everybody at the other
restaurant."

I wanted to laugh; this one was too easy to read.

I decided to open him up like a can of worms. Maybe I had some
of Healer's teachings running through my head because I peeled Ferrari
Man like a freshly picked grape. He told me things that made the tables
full of interested two-tops around us strain into listen to.

His longest relationship was a year and a half. For a man well into
his fifties, this spoke volumes. I asked him about his childhood and he
told me he moved constantly, sometimes in the middle of a school year,
so he could not even say goodbye to his friends. During his formative
years, he moved every year and a half.

I inquired if he had ever made the correlation between his childhood moves and the duration of his women. He said yes, indeed, it occurred to him a couple years back. (Or one point five women ago). It
took him almost fifty years to figure this out? Right, maybe I shouldn't be
talking quite yet, as there was a lot that I was still learning about myself.
No judgements with Ferrari Man, this was just his story.

He found me interesting enough to try to win me over. He suggested we plan weekend getaways, further painting the picture of the
fun ride with Ferrari Man. With this man, it was expiration dating at its
finest, and I knew the time frame, so no thank you. After getting a bit
of wine in him, and maybe sensing that he was losing me, Ferrari Man
made his final ploy and told me about his sexuality. He told me about the
first woman he was with and how she had taught him how to be a great
lover. He explained how he enjoyed bringing women to orgasm over and
over and how nothing pleased him more. He actually gave me a list of
six things all men need to do to be great in bed.

I found his list fascinating enough to write down. This one may have
had a screw loose, but he also had some interesting ideas about screwing.
Ferrari Man's List:

1. Sex is ninety percent in your head (Okay, we must have been
    reading the same books).

166

2. It is necessary to use all senses: sight, sound, touch, smell, and taste.

3. Men have to give one hundred percent of themselves, focusing on the woman in order to get their reward.

4. Mirror the woman's breath when she has an orgasm, mock her breathing and it will intensify her moment.

5. Find her trigger point. Be relentless in the search. Every woman has something that pushes her button (i.e. pulling their hair, saying something, sweet nothings at the right moment, grabbing her waist). Finding the trigger point is fun and essential!

6. Every time a woman has an orgasm, a man should have a mental orgasm.

I was impressed; Ferrari Man was clearly into the fine art of sexual pleasure. I took in this conversation like a girl on an expedition, considering it pure research. Sex is interesting and fascinates me, the why of it all. I mean, everyone is seeking something slightly different from sex. The list is endless: validation, love, pleasure, procreation, reassurance, comfort, reward, and duty may even fall on a list or two.

After our appetizer, wine, and the sex tutorial, we hopped back into his Ferrari and made the quick jaunt to my car. He was flying high off the thought of making me his next year-and-a-half gal, and I was still processing how unique this evening was. He told me his lips looked just like Elvis', and he wanted to serenade me with them. Well, what could I say?

I sat in his parked car, with a polite smile planted on my face, as he broke into a ballad, joining Elvis blaring from his high-end sound system. His voice was battling it out with the music in an all-out war. Ferraris are small, and there was nowhere to go. I plastered on my best "mom face" as I observed him. I saw him at that moment like a small child, showing me what he could do. I bit the side of my mouth as he hit his finest notes. I should have been an actress; I was impressed with my starring role as a spectator.

Ferrari Man then leaned in to kiss me. I confess, I knew this man was not for me, but my sense of curiosity came through—would he actually be decent? So I kissed back.

He stopped mid-kiss and asked if he could rub my feet. It must have been Elvis, because off went my shoes. He proceeded to do a mediocre job at a foot massage. He then put my foot into his mouth and bit it ever so slightly.

Disturbingly, and to my shock, this sent a wave of pleasure pulsing throughout my body. It also sent off an alarm bell in my head. Time to go! He put my foot down after the bizarre gnawing event and leaned in to kiss me again. Yuck, my mouth, his mouth, my foot, our mouths. I politely allowed one last, closed-mouth kiss and headed for the hills. Grabbing my shoes at lightning speed, I darted for my car.

"Thank you!" soared out of my violated lips. My car unlocked, the engine started, and my ass flew onto the familiar seat.

I was home within moments. I ran upstairs and sat on the edge of my bathroom sink to soak my feet in hot water. I washed the evening off in privacy.

SPECIAL OPS

"All you need for a movie is a gun and a girl."
—JEAN-LUC GODARD

THIS ONE FALLS INTO THE CATEGORY OF WHAT WAS I THINKING? I saw Special Ops online. He rattled on about polo ponies and travel in his bio. He lived in a town that I adored that also hosted my daughter and favorite son-in-law. He had a twinkle in his eye that reflected his intelligence and wit. Special Ops proclaimed he was looking for one woman; it all added up. After a couple of great phone conversations, I decided to take a leap of faith, drive three hours north to Santa Barbara, and get myself a hotel room to go meet this guy.

Santa Barbara was a place I loved, and, if worse came to awful, I could go see my daughter and her hubby. This was going to cost me a couple of bucks, but my heart was ready for a new adventure and that could involve some risk.

I met Ops at a restaurant in Montecito, an exclusive town close to Santa Barbara that hosts wealthy residents such as Oprah. Over dinner, he told me he had been a child prodigy and was speaking German by age eight. Friends of the family saw that he could further his studies in college and dragged him off to master the language. So, at age ten, he took a German language college course.

I know it sounds like a crock, but I believed him. Maybe I'm too gullible? After dinner, we went to visit his home that sat on a hill over-looking beautiful Santa Barbara. He had surveillance cameras in every room and a special police CB radio going off at all times to see if any-one needed assistance.

This whole encounter felt really weird. He told me he was in gov-ernment Special Forces and was planted in Germany as a secret agent. Again with the . . . *what*? Do ex-spies tell people they are ex-spies?

Please understand, I am a yoga girl; all peace, love, acceptance, fruit, nuts, granola, and kale, preferably blended in a morning smooth-ie. This guy was not only waiting for World War III, he was armed for it. On Saturday, we chugged around town in his army-camouflaged truck (note: he also had a Bentley) as I was literally sitting on a loaded gun, conveniently placed under the foam seat.

We could not have been more opposite. He offered to take me to the range to go shooting. Why not? When in Rome. As it turned out, I was a brilliant shot. Must have been the yoga.

He kept saying, "You killed that guy."

I'd shoot again and he'd repeat, "You killed that guy."

It was beginning to freak me out.

The best I could ever do before this date would be lead a yoga practice, followed by mindful meditation.

Halfway through the shooting range date, I made a lame excuse and headed back home as fast as possible. I believe I sped. I was be-ginning to get spooked and had to, once again, reevaluate my choices.

Yogi Barbie girl meets GI Joe—there's a reason these toys sit on different shelves.

Welcome to the wonderful world of online dating! May the next interesting fellow please step forward. I loved the fact that I had not given up on dating and adopted a boatload of rescue cats. After all, a meet and greet like that can make your head spin.

I knew the right man was out there for me. There are, in fact, many great single men in the world. Tons, droves, scores, it's just a mat-ter of finding the right fit. My online profile went up, and then down, up, then down. I was back online like a kid in a bounce house, but with way better outfits.

Man-Ifesting a Man

"Every great work, every big accomplishment, has been brought into manifestation through holding to the vision, and often just before the big achievement, comes apparent failure and discouragement."

—Florence Scovel Shinn

My arsenal of love guidance includes, but is not limited to, laws of attraction, setting personal intentions, prayer, and a gut-deep belief that the love of my life is en route. I kept myself busy and happy. In many ways, I have been preparing for this mystery man to man-i-fest. Even though years have rolled by, should I give up?

I have been busy with a minor home makeover, getting rid of things that are tired and have seen more than I should ever admit. Thank you, Star Dresser, for jump starting that process for me. I am content knowing that my memory mattress may hold memories, but grateful it mocks me in silence.

I have been on a tangent trying to get my house dolled up. I decided to get a new couch. I was looking for a comfy "man" style type, one made of black leather that reclines all the way into heaven. I *had* to be able to snare a man with such a fine piece of furniture. I asked the salesman at the furniture store to find me a six-foot-plus man to try it on for size. He inquired if I had such a man waiting for me at home. I told him I was buying the couch based on the field of dreams theory: buy the couch and the man will show up. He gave me a sideways glance, like a puppy straining to understand.

On a very warm summer weekend, I bought some cottage white paint and started painting the family room that would one day host my man-couch. I rocked out with the Beach Boys blaring in the background. Okay, I will confess, it was not Beach Boys. I was listening to the Shrek movie soundtrack, Shrek and Shrek 2.

I ended up peeling off my top, and what remained was a black bra paired with stretchy yoga pants. I love to paint! My poor slate floor became more freckled by the moment, and my bra soon looked like it had auditioned for 101 Dalmatians: The Sexy Sequel.

Sadly, the only audience participation throughout this show were a couple of dogs that kept a safe distance from the rapidly zooming paint spatters. If I had popcorn and beer, I could have sold tickets. The now infamous paint-spattered-bra will always remind me that I can make changes when I put my mind to it. It empowers me with the same magic as Superman's cape, however, in a more supportive role.

I was desperately trying to create peace and order to avoid sabotaging any future love opportunity with disorganization or hyperactivity. Star Dresser had helped me, yet remnants of my absent-minded personality were still intact.

Getting organized is crucial, as I'm the type of gal that often finds missing thong underwear in pant legs. Oh, and who was the brilliant person that figured out combining pantyhose and jeans could help rock a look?

I had painted walls and received my yoga teaching certificate. My closet had clothes that were ready for dating. My bras outnumbered my shoes. Some guy would love that.

I had exhausted all my resources and energies. I made changes from the inside out. Now it was time to sit back and see what would happen. Stay tuned.

Phone A Friend

"We are so happy to advise others that occasionally we even do it in their interest."

—Jules Renard

IN A FIT OF OBSESSING OVER PAST LOVES, I CALLED OREGON GUY. He was whip-smart, made me laugh, and always provided a much-needed male perspective. I whined on and on about how I kept getting caught in the same pickle. He listened with the patience of a doctor, until he didn't. He had his fill of my complaints and spontaneously pounced on me. He hit me upside the head with his words.

"Stop doing what you're doing. It's not working!" Snapping at me, that was his first bit.

"Write down all these men and draw a parallel. You are the common thread!"

"You may see all these dudes as different, but **trust** me, they are *not*. Why did you choose them? How did they make you feel? What did you like about them?"

While Oregon Guy continued, I took notes like, "Date against your type," and finally, "Figure out what part you played in all of this. It is about *you*, not *them*."

Lessons to be absorbed, for sure. Was it all about me? Did this all happen *to* me? Or did this happen *for* me? Any instance where I can learn, grow, and do better was happening *for* me. All of my experiences had jewels of lessons, if I wanted to be brave enough to see them. No victims allowed in this row, please move up into the nosebleed section.

I love Oregon Guy; his outlook on life had always made me laugh. I have always held him dear to my heart.

After our phone conversation, I followed his advice to the letter. I wrote down a list of men's names, quickly coming to an astounding revelation about myself. It took all of three minutes to unravel many years and the mystery of my choices. Three minutes! After decades of running in circles, my freeing realization came rapidly to me. I didn't have to dig too deep. The answer had been right there all along, just like Dorothy's red ruby slippers.

Subconscious repetition is when I choose a man who is unavailable to me in some way again and again. The million-dollar question is why? I realized that I have been overly available for all of these men to the point of unflattering pursuit, like with Lover. I could sit down and analyze my relationship with my father, but I've already done that, with a skilled therapist. It wasn't that. Like a nut falling from the tree, it finally hit me on the head. The only two men I was ever really close with, and experienced deep and intimate love with, had both pursued me. One relationship ended in betrayal, and the other berated my spirit. I was making choices to avoid that without even knowing it!

By George, I've got it! I had equated being pursued as unsafe. Without knowing it, I was choosing men that would not pursue me. So presto, I went straight for the unavailable man. He was not going to pursue me, he was unavailable! Bingo, I was tripping up in my own familiar. It was all neatly and deeply hiding under the surface, somewhere nearby but not fully aware, that dark little place where my wounds lived. My behavior had been well organized, and currently, astonishingly obvious.

Wow! Now what? I held the key to unlock the door, was I just going to stand in front of it? Uh, maybe . . . it could be scary on the other side. Change versus the familiar, I must bravely move away from this pattern and into the unknown.

It felt like my only chance.

I began by giving myself positive affirmations, inventing my own mantras: "I am worthy of an available man to pursue and cherish me."

It is easier said than done. Mantra on.

"I am excited to meet him, and he will pursue me and adore me."

The most important mantra of all, "I will not chase after him." Or was that one a stern warning?

HEALER AND MY HEALING

"Did I offer peace today? Did I bring a smile to someone's face? Did I say words of healing? Did I let go of my anger and resentment? Did I forgive? Did I love? These are the real questions. I must trust that the little bit of love that I sow now will bear many fruits, here in this world and the life to come."

—HENRI NOUWEN

HEALER HAS ALWAYS GENTLY PUSHED ME IN THE RIGHT DIRECtion. Unlike the loving brutality of Oregon Guy, Healer is sweeter in her style. She is very gifted at guiding and knows on a spirit level what is truly in one's best interest. I was without a man at the moment, and this was just what I needed.

Healer and I sat down for a much-welcomed healing session. Her kind intentions for my happiness and her insight were a winning combination.

I needed to forgive myself and the painful choices I had made. I had to look at myself with compassion and lift up the girl in me that had been anxiously trapped in fear and pain. The girl who truly did not feel worthy of love. My sad history pulsed through my veins. On a deep, unseen level, I believed I was the girl worthy of being abandoned.

Healer dug up what I had been fiercely trying to hide. She then assisted me, shining a light into my personal dark convictions. That light allowed the fears to be noticed, forever helping me to become aware, to become awakened. This was intense, and with her support, not scary at all.

I can have great love. I am worthy of great love. I do love myself, and it was safe to embrace all of my journey.

I can quite easily forgive, love, and pray for others. When it comes to showing myself the same favor, I faltered. I had put myself in hurtful situations, and that was no one's fault but my own. I had repeatedly stood in front of the unavailable men begging and pleading for their love. After Healer's enlightenment, I realized I had to be careful not to attach myself to the same tired belief system that had been driving my past.

Healing Through Feelings

"Your feelings so are important to write down, to capture, and to remember because today you're heartbroken, but tomorrow you'll be in love again."

—Taylor Swift

Putting on my big girl panties, I decided to take a couple of months away from dating to reflect on Oregon Guy's welcomed male perspective and the recent work I did with Healer. I was past many men including Big and Exception; this was my interim. I walked, did yoga, wrote in my journal, painted, and gardened. I turned down hanging out with my guy friends and just settled down with myself. It felt quiet and good.

Keeping a gratitude journal has always been vital for me. I can always find something to be grateful for, even when life is full of heart-ache. It helps me to find healing and blessings in moments that suck. It is magical how pulling in the positive creates a shift out of a funk or woeful journey. Stepping toward courage, one better thought at a time.

It is important to be aware of all feelings, be it good or bad. Being aware of my feelings, even when it is pain, anger, or disappointment is essential for me, and is better than denying and coming unhinged.

I learned this lesson the hard way as my stuffed feelings of anger

177

surfaced and turned into a kidney infection back when I was dating Six. My body got "pissed" for me, as I writhed in pain.

Six had no qualms about expressing his anger; it flew from him rapidly, loud and without hesitation. I ducked, covered, and sadly cowered.

I was not going to get near anger, it scared the crap out of me. It seemed as if I was too stifled to express my feelings. I did not have a voice or a way to let out what took years to build up. My body expressed itself in the worst way. It expressed what my words did not yet have the capacity to do. I became ill.

My mantras became:

"I will acknowledge when I feel angry. It is safe expressing anger in a way that is healthy for me."

"It is okay to feel anger."

"I have a right to feel anger."

At this point in my life, I began working hard at recognizing my feelings. I aimed to discover where they were in my body and if they were ready to shift. It seemed that if I simply allowed myself to feel whatever feeling it is, like sadness for example, it leaves much faster. I talked right to my sadness as if it was lovingly listening to me.

I would say, "Oh there you are Sadness; you're the size of a grapefruit in my tummy. Where did you come from? Can I send you out with love? How about if we shrink down your size? Okay, thank you, you're a bit smaller just for the asking. I see you, I feel you. I am aware you are here, but you are temporary, I will feel better soon. I have every right to feel you, Sadness, but one day you will be a distant memory. I must now go about my day."

Only then would I be alright with having Sadness follow me around, because I was strongly aware of the fact that it was just a temporary state I needed to function through. I never embraced those moments as who I was, just what I was going through.

LESSONS

"You have to learn the rules of the game. And then you have to play better than anyone else."
—ALBERT EINSTEIN

I LEARNED FROM LOVER NOT TO CHASE. MEN MUST CHASE AFTER me, and, uh, I want them to chase me. I learned from Big that I want a future and an open line of communication. I learned from Exception that it is high time to exit the playground. Recess is over. I learned from Dream Mate that the best place to be is in the arms of your best friend, honesty required. Benefit taught me I would rather have exclusivity and love. With Beebe, I learned it is safe to be treated like a Queen. With Six, I learned it is vital to speak my truth and stand in my strength. Perhaps, where I have rested my head has brought me to a closer understanding of myself. Would somebody please hand me an effing PhD already?

My thighs hold many truths and have done much research.

Dating Spin Cycle

"That's the awful thing about dating. Tight underwear. We would all like to be in a big bra and pants and when you are in a secure relationship, you can do that."

—Dawn French

THE JUGGLING ACT OF MEETING MEN CAN QUICKLY GET OUT OF control. I sincerely lacked organization. I managed my system by storing men into my phone by their first name, the town they lived in, and the place we were meeting.

I knew this was kind of awful; I could hear myself.

For example, listed in my phone: 'Scotty-SB-Fred-Fest'. Lord, help me! This was the method I had come up with! I would love to just have one guy, work, cell, and home. How sweet would that be? How sweet will that be!

One of my guy friends told me the pathway to hell is paved with women like me that sort out their men in such demeaning manners. I saw it as hanging onto a thread of organization, but, guilt raised its head, and I started to delete phone numbers and clean up my act. I would be a good girl and wait for the one worthy man. He just had to figure out how wonderful I was, dammit.

During one recent date with a seemingly smart guy, he told me that men are like go-carts: simple pull start, gas, brake, turn. Women are like high-end cars with all the whistles and gadgets imaginable. If a part breaks down on said girl-car, it is costly and has to be specially shipped, packed with the utmost white-gloved care, with a second team of white-gloved experts standing by for repair. Men, or go-carts, on the other hand, are simple, stop, go, and turn. He added that women were forever complicated, considering the precision of care required to maintain one. I may have had to agree with him to some degree.

Another guy friend of mine came up to me at a party after downing a bit of tequila. Standing in front of me, kind of puffing out his chest, he said, "I am all man. Do you know what that is?"

"Uh, no . . . do tell!" I said

"If we can't kill it, eat it, drive it, fuck it, or drink with it, we are not interested." He continued, feeling all manly, "Furthermore, if we're fucking it, we want to kill to eat and drink with the one we are fucking."

It was all so simple. Had I missed this basic caveman logic all along, or was I just beginning to understand now?

THE PSYCHIC

"The power of intuitive understanding will protect you from harm until the end of your days."

—LAO TZU

I AM A SKEPTIC. I AM A BELIEVER. I HAVE HAD MY OWN PSYCHIC moments, visions and otherworldly occurrences, yet I am still very leery. Healer can see beyond what is possible with supernatural insights. The awakening process is a powerful type of healing on a soul level. It can assist you in remembering your soul purpose in life and kick start your God-given gifts, bringing balance to the mind-body-spirit connection.

Healer is an Awakener.

Faith in the unseen has always been my heart's calling on some level. The dance between logic and the unknown is a human plight as well as a human light.

Perhaps my faith should carry me. Perhaps my faith does? I mostly trust that these otherworldly messages that are received come in through many methods, different cultures and religions, in all parts of the world. We are all humans in spirit-filled bodies.

I met with Psychic at Healer's house on a Sunday afternoon in the summer. We had a one-on-one appointment that lasted just shy of an hour. I was determined to reel in my personality and give her nothing, in a dopey attempt to hide from her. She had a private moment in prayer and then magically spoke words to me that I knew could only come from the inexplicable. She quickly told me many things with great detail. As I became intent on her words, I softened my attitude and I began to understand what a special moment this was for me.

I sat on a sofa across from Psychic with my legs folded cross-legged on my lap. Psychic sat facing me in a comfy chair with her feet planted on the ground. She was a very pretty, petite blonde, that I later found out had raised her twin boys mostly on her own. The warmth of her sweet nature was felt in the room. I loved her the moment I saw her; I just couldn't help it. She was as sweet as sweet can be, and it vibrated all around her like a golden light.

I felt a bit nervous not knowing what to expect. At the same time, an unusual calm came over me, and I was filled with a peace that surpassed my limited understanding. From this peaceful moment on, I just wanted to know more. I was excited like a kid on a perfect playground. I also wanted to know her. How could I not? She was mystically marvelous, wrapped in a blue summer dress. I felt a strong friend-love connection with her but kept those thoughts at bay so she could focus on her job.

Psychic was gifted in this unique talent and had been doing readings for fifteen years. I was more than impressed. She told me she was on the brink of obtaining her PhD in clinical psychology focusing on social work, specializing with trauma patients.

I witnessed her effortlessly dive into an enchanted trance as a thick Irish accent emerged from her petite body. It was very strange, but I was unnaturally comfortable with this Irish change in her delivery. My importance seemed international.

She gave me great details about a man that would be entering my life at some point. "He is on his way. You will know him right away. He is a lover of cars, and he has many. The bed you share is carved wood, maybe from Italy."

She continued on in this new Irish inflection that somehow suited her, "A feeling of certainty will prevail."

Psychic said that the greatest desire in my heart was directed toward a relationship.

I was insistent on knowing more about Lover. She said "Oh, he is an expert in money and financing." Duh.

She was emphatic, "He is not the one."

I squirmed, wanting him to be the one. I protested, insisted, and embarrassed myself by questioning what she had already been very clear about.

Like a small child wanting my way, I argued with her, "No! I really like him, he has deep pockets and a big cock!"

This made her giggle, and her delight filled the room. I loved to make people laugh, but I continued to force the issue while willing my desired outcome.

Psychic laughed. "No, my love, he is not the one," she said, repeating herself with the patience of a kindergarten teacher.

She told me, "Your souls and bodies are attracted to one another, even your minds are attracted."

Psychic continued, "He might circle back around. Your connection may come back around. I see that it is important for you to keep him as a friend."

Again, she was correct. It was important to me that we remained friends. She saw my disappointment and gently continued, "The 'one' is on his way. You have not met him yet."

How could I be disappointed with this news? I was as happy for myself as I was sad. After all, Lover and I had stepped away from one another.

I wanted to chalk it up to a beautiful story, but I knew that would be unwise. I decided to embrace this reading and focus on what Psychic had revealed to me. Think about it. When someone meets with you in a blue summer dress, speaks in an accent, and tells you fabulous things about yourself, you just go with it. Duh.

Within a moment of silence and great certainty, I became profoundly aware that all the people that had entered my life had become my guideposts. I was the type of person that could easily turn at the drop of a hat and jet off in any given direction. I was a spontaneous creature and always trusted the outcome of my decisions, with a strong belief that life was on my side.

I had deep gratitude for those who had come into my life. Ones who had loved me and I had loved in return. When my heart is open to Spirit, I can get the lessons wherever I turn.

Yoga had helped me to become grounded. My yoga teacher taught me to be still, to accept, and to listen. I taught her to have fun like a child dancing free from onlookers. Both are lessons from the inside out.

Pink Eraser

"Tomorrow is always fresh, with no mistakes in
it."

—Lucy Maud Montgomery,
AUTHOR OF *Anne of Green Gables*

ONE NIGHT, AFTER A SWEET DINNER WITH Piano Player AND HIS
family, I started to head home.

My favorite little four-year-old ran across the room yelling after
me.

"Wait, I have something for you, Auntie!"

I stopped and bent down to give her my full attention, asking,
"What is it?"

Her bright blue eyes, full of wonder, sought my reaction. In her
tiny palm was a rectangular pink block. "It's an eraser," she said. "Now
you don't *ever* have to worry about *any* of your mistakes!"

It's astounding how children can change our lives with their simple
truth. Clenching my new gift in the palm of my hand, I scooped up that
little angel and gave her one last hug before I left. That moment was as
simple as my heart would allow it to be.

"Thank you! I will always keep this with me." And I did.

Now that I had an eraser, I no longer had to worry about my flubs!
This felt like the best gift I had gotten my entire life. I mean, it's the

key to the golden city. After that moment, I realized worrying about my screw-ups and my pathway down dark roads would never help me heal. I would just erase them and allow the magical pink rubber dust to fall from my blunder; it's over. I thanked God for my friends, even the pint-sized ones.

New chances come with each day. Every morning I must decide whether to start out in prayer and gratitude, or worry and fret. Life is ever-changing and can oftentimes dictate growth. Denial and I had held hands and skipped through a great deal together, bombarding our way through repression, covering up many a-truths with a multitude of things trapping myself in the familiar.

Would I rather continue hanging out with my old friend denial? That tired relationship never assists with healing. It brings about procrastination, which is a sickness that fosters stagnation. The ugly head of refusal raises itself, and the blinders no longer serve their intended purpose. Like a sharp and painful slap in the face, reality comes as an appalling feeling, but it also brings sweet relief. I remind myself to face the tough stuff. I must change my thoughts, hop onto a different road, hopefully one that is on the corner of Now and Gratitude.

TRY, TRY AGAIN

"If at first you don't succeed, try, try again. Then quit. There's no point in being a damn fool about it."

—W. C. FIELDS

WHILE REFLECTING ON TWO DECADES OF DATING, OR NOT DATING, and looking at my choices, I do sit back with some regret. How can I not? I have stumbled and fallen right into the wrong relationships. I am also well aware that some of the men I have passed over may have been worthy. Was it me and my tattered history that lead me to leave behind some good ones while feverishly chasing after the wrong ones?

I look at these men now and kick myself from here to next Sunday. Smart, successful, loyal, sexy, and, uh, adored me, or so I thought. Oklahoma and Oregon came to mind, and some beyond these pages. Perhaps it was timing? Many things factor in when it comes to love. Looking at it now is like analyzing personal love data.

Waiting for what is behind door number two is foolish and folly. What's behind the curtain? Oh, that's right, it's the Wizard of Oz! I can't date him, he has a funny voice, and his hair is pretty done up. How can I behave so fussily when I am, in fact, flawed? Was I just hoping for the next best thing? Was I behaving in a way that would always keep me at arm's length from my dream?

I muster up a positive self-talk.

Be in the moment. Be happy, see the joy, and veer from too quick to no. I must remember to love the one I'm with: me. That is foremost. Lean toward yes and possibilities. I have a pink eraser: I can do it!

Oh my, I feel a mantra coming on:

"I accept the choices I have made. I am learning from my own precious history."

LOVER AGAIN

"All the dreamers in all the world are dizzy in the noodle."

—EDIE ADAMS

CIRCLING BACK AROUND, EXPECTING THE UNEXPECTED, ALL THIS seems to be true, especially with Lover.

Recycling, isn't that good for the environment?

Coming back around to a lover gone by, is that so wrong? Lest I judge myself, or judge others that have fallen into the alluring comfort of the once known.

Moreover, in my "reading" with Psychic, she indicated that Lover and I might return to each other. Reasoning that I would not be adding to my "numbers," I quickly found comfort in finding pleasure.

Or was I just the dumb-ass that was returning for more of the same torture? When would I learn?

Lover had *finally* broken up with his girl. He sent her packing with a parting gift valued at a couple hundred thousand, or so he said. He seemed pretty torn up, but, like a knee-jerk reaction, over to my house he went. As he stood in front of me, I wanted to fall into his arms, into his warm hug. He smelled like fresh soap.

I was empty nesting and was insistent on finding a new life outside of my home and raising my children. I had to find myself beyond being a single parent.

I was having a hot tub delivered to my home, getting my home ready to put on vacation rental listings. It was late spring, and I had guests booked in a matter of weeks. Lover helped roll the new hot tub in though the tight fit of the front gate. He suggested that I meet him at his new place in Rancho Santa Fe.

Rancho Santa Fe is filled with perfectly landscaped ranch properties that roll on from one estate to the next. It is home to pampered, shiny horses living like fat cats, placed behind rolling green pastures and framed with white-lined fences. I loved this town.

I was wide-eyed at the suggestion to go visit him at his new home, as I felt some kind of business was not quite done with us. A heart that was naive and searching hopped into the car and headed south to see my once Lover. I believe my heart was doing the driving.

Or it could have been the thought that great sex was awaiting. It would have then been my pants doing the driving, and I'm not sure if they have a valid driver's license.

This time around, a grain of salt was added to our relationship—I would not bawl my eyes out over him. If I wanted to play with this man, I needed to adhere by the rules. The truth for me depended on me wanting it to be different—I had to stop that. I always over-analyzed the crap out of things, with some false sense of reasoning and weak-minded chatter covering for my inexcusable choices.

And yet I couldn't ignore the fact that pleasure of the loveliest kind did await me in Lover's arms. If it wasn't served with a side of false hope, I would have been a more balanced human.

Finding the private gate was tricky, but it opened for me upon entering the code. The driveway curved around rich landscape that went on for nearly a mile. It was "country private" at its finest, chiseled out for the wealthy. Lover's surroundings were tropical and lush, but he complained the wildlife was a threat to his puppy family. Mountain lions, bobcats, and coyotes ran amok on his many acres.

I walked up the stone path into a courtyard with an infinity pool, back house, and patio area landscaped with vines and flowers, where the smell of jasmine hung in the air. I felt like I walked into a scene from an Italian movie with overgrown tropical plants.

Entering the main house through the glass sliders, the ceiling soared way too high above my head. It felt like stepping into a cathedral. I didn't know if I should look up or gaze upon my once upon a time Lover as he approached me.

Lover's home in Rancho Santa Fe was over-the-top, dated, lavish, and cold. There were many remnants of architectural ideas that never materialized, like a wandering koi pond that spread throughout a couple of rooms but was temporarily boarded up with plywood. It all felt awkward and confusing: a random fireplace stood in the middle of the hallway, a fountain was built into what was to be an indoor courtyard, and bathrooms were way too large with inoperative bidets. Bidets are wonderful toilets that you sit on and they spray your behind clean with warm water. The bidet was as out of place as I was.

Was this home to code?

Lover's home felt strange and funky, and, if I didn't have such affection for Lover, I would have gotten the hell out of there. I had the feeling that if I stayed, I would somehow get lost, like in a horror movie. My body would be found months later, eaten by the return of killer koi fish, discovered by a startled housekeeper with cold, vacant eyes. It was a dreadful home with no soul.

This home gave me a creepy feeling and I didn't know why. Did this weird home factor into their break? I needed to focus on us not them. I was beginning to understand why Lover was so hell-bent on getting out of there. Bad mojo was lurking in the corners. I had to remind myself that I had come to see Lover, and, oh, to get laid.

I really just wanted to get laid.

Determined to have a good time with Lover, I bucked up and readied for bed. We had great naked playtime.

Yippee, I got laid.

However, when it came to sleeping, I could not relax. I crammed myself over to his side of the bed where he was just clinging onto the edge, nearly falling onto the floor. I was searching for a false sense of protection. I felt bad knowing I ruined his sleep. Our playtime encounter in bed was spot on, but the vital sleep part of it was really messed up.

We both got out of bed cranky.

All of the food in the house was packed, even the coffee. I looked at the cans in the cupboard with great despair. I can do nothing with that.

Poor Lover, I understood why he moved less than a week later. An eerie, uneasy vibe resounded throughout his strange, opulent home. I'm glad I never went back to visit.

Lover was getting his Bentley painted, and we chatted about me driving it to his new home. He felt four weeks was too long for us to not see each other. I stupidly questioned myself, did we have a shot this time? He appeared overly ready to see me again.

Katie L. Lindley

It seemed I had not learned my lesson once again and accepted second place. That was no place for me to be.

I wanted more.

TIBURON

"Anyone who doesn't have a great time in San Francisco is pretty much dead to me."
—ANTHONY BOURDAIN

LOVER HAD PACKED UP ALL HIS WORLDLY POSSESSIONS, HIS numerous pups included. He was heading north for a new life away from his breakup, away from his failed attempt at a life with his new girl in Rancho Santa Fe. Lover had the funds to plunk down just about anywhere, so he decided to land in Tiburon, a pricey, exclusive peninsula that sits south of Sausalito. It overlooks the San Francisco Bay like a jewel watching its every sparkling moment.

I felt apprehensive about visiting Lover. I wondered, was there more awkward sleeping in store for us?

I batted away those thoughts and focused on the positive. I was grateful for this opportunity to spend more time with Lover. Yet, I was feeling confused, wondering where Lover and I had gone wrong on our last encounter.

Did he possess the bad mojo? Was this all a big mistake? Was I Lover's classic rebound babe? Never mind the classic rebound babe part, was I his on-demand rebound babe?

I found myself beat up over the last sad ending of us. Dear Lord, what was wrong with me? I questioned myself once again. My pattern, there it was, my old friend. My pattern was spiraling down toward my own vicious cycle, like a mangy dog chasing its tail. When would I exhaust myself to the point of collapse?

We agreed to get together as soon as his Bentley was painted. I was to drive it up to his new home on the bay. His Bentley was going to take way too long getting a fancy paint job, which required taking his car apart. Lover wanted to see me before that, so, one more time, I jumped.

With my devious lady business doing the legwork, I quickly planned a trip to Oregon, booking flights to see my gal pals and have some much-needed girl time. What a perfect excuse to dash down and see Lover.

Yippee, this was my kind of sex-drive, or would that be sex-flight?

Flying one thousand miles north to see my gal pals made me excited; knowing I was ending the trip with Lover left me feeling even better. I had a nonstop stellar visit with my friends in Oregon. I did a bit of bragging that I was getting on a plane to see my Lover. I mean, these rock star Oregon girls were planted in that state. A California girl flying about to see her Lover is pretty fancy. If one of those gals had a lover, he'd be in a nearby town.

I put on the perfect plane outfit, had washed hair, and was neatly packed. I may have had over-anticipated my casual visit with Lover.

He did not come to meet me at the airport but did have a driver waiting for me. That felt special, seeing a man in a black cap with a little cardboard sign with my name. It was shy of wonderful—perfect would have been Lover minus the hat.

The dude with the sign was welcomed. I needed to adjust my expectations.

The car was clean and had a large leather backseat I was able to rest on all the way to Tiburon. Driving through San Francisco, one of my favorite cities, I tried to take it in with every glance out the window. This was already a blast!

Lover greeted me in the front yard and seemed rather happy to see me. After whipping out cash and handing a wad to my driver, he grabbed my bag and ushered me in. I had a reunion with the dogs, who may have been a wee bit happier to see me than Lover.

Lover carried my duffel bag and easily plunked it down in the guest room. Okay, I should have gotten that memo because our vision for the weekend was skewed.

I looked at him with incredulous eyes and said with my this-is-how-it-is voice, "My bags can stay here, but I'm sleeping with you."

He did not argue and allowed me into his bed with his pups.

I gave him no choice. The perfect host obliged.

After he showed me about his home and the grounds, we sat on his bed, admiring the San Francisco Bay. Alcatraz Island was in the background, and it looked like a proud statement plunked down in the freezing water as we relaxed on his bed admiring it.

Behind Alcatraz was a city view of San Francisco. It was to be marveled at. After sunset, the city lit up like well-orchestrated fireflies in the night. Even the fog that rolled in was romantic.

On the right side of Lover's view was the Golden Gate Bridge, forever whimsical and enchanting. I was mesmerized by the beauty that Lover had placed himself into.

Right before dawn, I experienced one of the most breathtaking sights I had ever seen. It was just as the sun crept in and the lights of the city faded that I realized magic was real, it was right before my eyes. It all seemed fairytale-like to me, like I was expecting background music and a glass slipper to appear.

I remember repeating to Lover and myself, "Wow darling, you've done well."

Since Lover had just moved in, he was still setting up his new home. We bounced about the city and throughout the outskirts of Marin County and bought things to give the place a new look. It was fun dolling up his home. Lover was a man with deep pockets that loved secondhand stores and jeans priced under twenty bucks.

I loved watching him trying on pants, what can I say? Witnessing how he had to move his love package about to manage into a new pair of jeans fascinated me. I once again pondered; how does he tote that about all day?

He ended up buying me a pillow and crisp new sheets for us to share. All was good in Tiburon.

Lover unsuccessfully interviewed housekeepers on one of the days I was there. The person he was looking for needed to come over three times a week and basically help manage his home and dogs. He asked me to help before the next gal arrived and then cleared out, so I could show her the home and explain the requirements of the job.

Being appointed such a task had a very "lady of the house" feel. Although I fell into this role with great ease, I knew this was only a temporary gig.

Lover landed on the gal I interviewed and hired her on the spot. It all seemed to work out perfect for him. I was glad in that moment I was able to help him and our friendship was going well.

I fell in love with Tiburon during my trip to see Lover. It was a perfect fit for me: the artsy town, salty culture, old homes, laid back vibe, peaceful hills ready for hikes, with water strewn on all sides. San Francisco was only a heartbeat away.

It did not take much to imagine Tiburon as my new home. I went on to wonder if, in fact, I could fall in love with Lover?

I then understood my love was for the town, not for Lover. Dang. Ugh, darn, damn! As Oregon Guy would say, "Ah fuckity-fuck."

After that trip, I could see why San Francisco was the city you leave your heart in.

Lover and I had a great time, and my trip was delightful in every way. He was good to me. We seemed to be each other's "in-between" people, not altogether flattering, yet we were happy and comfortable when together instead of alone. We had created a connection for certain and probably for life, a fondness, a kinship.

Lover was not my guy. It is hard to explain how I knew he was not my guy, but he just wasn't. He was a great guy, but not mine. I would have loved it to be different, but it wasn't.

Our likes and dislikes contradicted one another. Lover started his morning with milk, cold cereal and donuts, while I preferred rice milk, or water with lemon followed by a kale smoothie. I enjoyed yoga, and he enjoyed walking his dogs and going fishing. I loved reading, but he never reads. I watched feel-good movies, and he always had CNN buzzing. He was forever aware of his finances, with a team of money managers, and I rarely even checked my bank balance. I loved music, and he loved the sound of his dogs' tails thumping and the stock market rising. I had grown children, while he had no children and a vasectomy.

I think I began grappling with these issues, wondering, "Why not us, why not now?"

Was it his love of donuts? Kale verses donuts, a ridiculous argument never to have.

Maybe I should have paid closer attention to his online profile details.

The Queen

"Think like a queen. A queen is not afraid to fail.
Failure is another stepping stone to greatness."
—Oprah Winfrey

As a Queen, I will step into what I need to with great confidence. I had an enormous "ah ha" moment. Who coined that phrase anyway, Oprah?

When I added together all of the men that had entered my life, they created one perfect man. All the men and all the purposes they had served me. They quickly all blurred into 'the one man' I had been looking for all along.

This was astounding, and yet I was not surprised in the least. Subconscious matter drives everyone, and I had ordered up my man based on a list of what would truly suit me. This list had come into my psyche long before the many men showed up. I *had* my one guy, except he was fragmented into several dudes.

I did not currently have the lover, which was surely on my list, and specific as well, lest I forget that! Duct tape and glue would not fuse these men into my one guy. I realized I couldn't create a Frankenstein-Love-Man out of fragmented parts, even though October was near.

Didn't I have a cauldron somewhere? I remembered one that sat next to my wand and broomstick! One man, not two, not a dozen, I just longed for one. One that suited me. Now it was a matter of using the broom to clean out the closet and ready myself for the one.

OFFLINE

"Learn from yesterday, live for today, hope for tomorrow. The important thing is not to stop questioning."

—ALBERT EINSTEIN

I DECIDED TO DISASSEMBLE MY ONLINE DATING PROFILE PERMA-nently. I needed a break from the virtual dating world. I decided I wanted to try something different, or at least stop trying what was not working. With that in mind, and two weeks left of my online dating membership, I headed for the final push, the last call. I threw lines out in many directions, said farewell to a handful of fellows, and attached my number to a couple more. All cyber connections.

My online profile was officially down! The history of my online men was enough to tally up and look back into the fragmented romances and frustrations. It seemed as if my picking abilities should have been questioned.

I experienced some withdrawals as I missed the false consideration that online dating provided. I won't lie, I was feeling the lack of attention.

I found myself returning to my computer to sort through all the mystery that it once held for me. My computer sat blank and blameless on my bed, haunting me, or was it mocking me?

Was I lacking the momentary attentiveness? Was I really that desperate that this nonthreatening online buzz was feeding my ego? Filling me up to some degree with a sense that I was desirable and worthy? Waiting for a flirt, wink, or like.

That premise is clearly stupid and sad. Online dating had been my go-to guilty pleasure, yet now my computer lay silent, as it should. I sat next to it, wanting it to feed me like a hungry puppy. Awful. Step away from the computer.

Luck With The Last?

"Even if I knew that tomorrow the world would
go to pieces, I would still plant my apple tree."
—Martin Luther

I RECENTLY HAD A DATE THAT WAS FAIRLY IDEAL. HE WAS ONE OF my last dates before I kicked out my online profile forever. He was handsome, smart, easygoing, and fun. We met at the spectacular Montage hotel for an event that honored investment bankers; the bank threw it.

I asked him, "So we are going to a party to celebrate rich people?"

I was relieved when he readily understood my humor.

It was extravagant, to say the least. Located inside, the party flowed to the outside, with crashing waves feet away—it felt elegantly relaxing and casual. I was in a scene from The Great Gatsby. They had staff walking around, white-gloved, and with pies on popsicle sticks.

Can you imagine? A bouquet of mini pies presented by good-looking men and women wearing tuxes? This brought a whole new challenge to Thanksgiving. Honestly, Martha Stewart would have been impressed. I would have steered her away from my date, though. He was pretty great.

My date was keenly interested in saying hello to the tellers that he dealt with often. I really liked that about him; he cared about his daily peeps. His favorite teller, Betty, came bouncing up to us, all bubbly, excited, and gussied up. She was delightful and engaging. She began to share with us her utter joy regarding a friend gifting her a collectible Barbie doll. That was her hobby.

I was amazed and inquired further. She gushed and went on about these nostalgic plastic wonders that held a place in her heart and described the many display cases scattered throughout her home.

I requested to see photos of them on her phone. Of course she had photos! Anyone who is nuts about something has numerous amounts of phone pictures. She trotted off to fetch her phone.

My date was speechless. He noticed I could blend in with any crowd and about any subject. Okay, so the subject matter wasn't foreign affairs. That would have made my drop jaw and drool, and not in a good way. In a, "Oh, uncle Freddie is asleep on the couch again" way. Barbie dolls, give it to me, I could take that on. I was obviously trying to impress my date.

Betty returned with her well-documented collection in hand. I told her, in front of my new guy, "I was always confused that Ken and Barbie both had vaginas."

She busted up. Hasn't everyone thought of that? I mean, Mattel made the bump, a blameless bump, but a bump just the same. Ken's bump mimicked Barbie's. I liked the male form, but as a small child, I was confused by his parts. I knew as a small tot where my happy place was. And according to the naked dolls, Ken's looked the same as mine.

After the party, we made our way upstairs to the lobby to see my friend Piano Man. He welcomed me over as we made our way to a comfy couch. Listening to Piano Man extended my time with my new date, and I felt happy about that. Piano Man chatted with us between sets; it was a near perfect evening. My date walked me to the valet where he paid the man and gave me a much-welcomed hug that lingered a moment or two longer than normal for a first date.

R2 and I just had our first date.

R2 Squared

"The game of life is a game of boomerangs. Our thoughts, deeds, and words return to us sooner or later with astounding accuracy."

—Florence Scovel Shinn

R2 stood about six foot two and a half, with dimples, and blue eyes—very all-American. He was well-studied in math and computer science. R2's full head of white hair had a hint of blond. The body that he worked out hard for was lean and fit, and I loved the way he smelled, like linen and fresh soap. At sixty, he looked forty, especially naked. I sometimes stared at his flawless skin in envy as mine was not half as nice as his. I hated that fact. We had both been told by our friends to date outside our "type," which is how we met. We were not each other's norm, yet somehow, we managed to look like we had walked out of a TV ad for couples weekly.

The memory of our magical night at the fancy Montage party was our wonderful first date story. After a handful of more sweetly innocent dates, he boldly proclaimed to me that he was "relationship ready." Hence R2 equaled relationship ready. He likened it to a math equation, which of course he did. That's what he said as we forged forward into an exclusive relationship, yippee.

Finally, a guy who wanted a relationship! This felt quite foreign, and I decided, without hesitation, to go for it. R2 was a wonderful, kind, smart, sexy, driven man. He professed that he was indeed looking for the "end game." What did that sound like to me? Had I heard a promise of a promise of a forever after? Hadn't I heard something like that before? I decided to shake off that feeling and be in the now.

What goes out of men's mouths and into women's ears can often become a wide-eyed serious game of assumption. I shouldn't get too ahead of myself.

I had never known anyone quite like R2. He was so good and kind to me that the unfamiliarity of it had me slightly off balance. He insisted on getting my door and the check. R2 was a true gentleman.

He was heading up one of the largest holistic alternative medical clinics throughout the country, one that would consequently have a profound global effect. This billion-dollar project that R2 had invested five years of his time into would be the first of its kind and was just getting going when I met him.

Needless to say, this project would become an all-consuming task that would subsequently keep him up at night, sweating out the details. I tried my best to champion him and his cause, reminding him of the untold thousands of lives he would forever be changing upon the project's inception. I had a deep understanding that I may not come first in his world at the time, and, with minor disappointment, I fully accepted the situation with R2.

R2 would constantly tell me that I made him feel calm when I was in his presence. This had never been told to me before that point. I am the type that tends to bounce from the inside out and with the capability of lifting a room's energy at any given time. My daughter laughed at this when I told her. She wondered how anyone could feel calm around me, ever.

Oregon Guy, cracking on me, didn't get it either. He said, "You're more like a five-hour energy drink. Just looking at you, I can see you bounce."

I finally had to ask my sweet R2 how this could be. He explained that he was so entrenched in his work and that being around me shifted his gears so he could focus on me and momentarily release his burdens. That was an explanation I understood. He saw me as whimsical and free. He could find joy in just that, lucky me. He was always fully present while with me. Whenever I was with him, I was fully happy.

R2 goes to Target every year after Thanksgiving and chooses a woman in line with no wedding ring and a cart full of gifts and food for her children. He then pays for her things, hands her a couple hundred dollars, and slips away.

Yes, I could love and appreciate a man such as this. Our intimacy and time together seemed to be slowly moving forward.

However, I had yet to meet his sons or brother. R2 never invited me to any of his business events, and I felt confused as to why. R2 had clearly compartmentalized me for the time being. In the long run, that would not work for me.

For a period of time, I accepted being R2's girlfriend. He was one of the funniest guys I had ever known. Just observing the hamsters spinning the wheels in his head was entertaining to me. He accepted my goofy side as well as my cranky moments.

I knew R2 loved me, although he never dared say it. So, with the lack of those three exquisite words, "I love you," I sensed a real fear of intimacy from him. I didn't judge him, but I knew it was there like the air we breathe.

I too felt a certain level of calmness settling in as I got to know R2. Yet weekends were spotty at best, an invisible barrier was clearly present between us. I began justifying all of my legitimate concerns in my relationship with R2, because, when I was with him, or even engaged in conversation with him, my heart found a home, a resting place that was humorous, peaceful, and sweet.

Hairpin Turn

"So much of life is luck. One day you make a right turn and get hit by a car. Turn left and you meet the love of your life. I think I made the correct turn."

—Loretta Swit

AFTER MONTHS OF MANY PROMISES, COUPLED WITH EXCUSES, R2 started to pull away. This fact hit me alongside a sinking feeling and great certainty. I found myself understanding what would happen next was somewhere between, "Oh Lord, here it comes" and "Oh no, there he goes."

My Spirit lead me to a beach I had visited many times before. I planted my feet in the friendly and familiar warm sand. I sensed a change as my heart wanted to break without knowing why, yet exactly knowing why. I felt R2 moving away from our relationship and stepping deeper into his cave. When someone in a relationship begins disengaging and backing away, it is always painful. I was being rejected. When I connect with a love, I have a bizarre sense of what their heart is doing. Like twins, I can sense things in the other person that are inexplicable.

R2 no longer wanted a relationship and all that that implied. Two days after my epiphany on the sand, he called me. I could tell by his tone that the breakup conversation was about to be delivered. I sat on

Katie L. Lindley

my bed, braced myself, and forgot to breathe.

He said, "I think we should end this." The sorrow in his voice was palpable.

"No, we don't need to," I replied.

This threw him off balance. He broke out into an uncomfortable laugh, unsure of how to respond. No girl had ever dished this one up to him.

"I don't think so buddy, not so fast," I said.

I am no ordinary girl and this was no ordinary moment.

I tried to explain myself, "I understand where you are in respect to the clinics and life right now. I have already experienced a shift in my head and heart that we have changed."

Carefully choosing my words, I proceeded, "I don't want the absence of you in my life. I am happy when I hear from you and when we spend time together. You do what you need to do, I'm not going anywhere. I understand the importance of your life's vision and fully accept where you are right now."

Accepting someone is real love. I was feeling it, and I was doing it. I knew I did not want him out of my life yet and that I had to have compassion for his project. I had to have compassion for him. I forgot to find compassion for myself. Maybe, in my honesty with him, I was not being honest with myself? Why was I fighting to keep him when he wanted to go?

I saw R2 the next day, and tears came rolling down his cheeks, surprised at the feelings he had for me. He sweetly referred to me as "Susan," the character on Seinfeld that would not let George break up with her. Susan's sad fate was death by poisonous envelope glue. He better had not imagined my ill-timed death by a bizarre poisonous mishap. I hope that was not a part of R2's forward thinking.

The fact of the matter remained that he was stepping back and that didn't feel good. I wanted that relationship, I wanted that endgame, I wanted *us*.

Having someone withdraw affection and step away from me was hurtful. I had been here before. The results of such a change inevitably pushes the other person out for mere survival. We tend to turn toward or away from our loved ones in this dance of life. It happens to some extent every day, and a subtle or severe maneuver can affect your human connection.

The question I needed to ask myself was, *could I let go of all the dreams I had attached to him?* Was I capable of shifting our romantic relationship into a friendship with R2? Or were we still dating? Had our status changed to dating? Did this imply we could date others?

This whole "breakup" but "let's not" deal had surely put us in an interesting state of uncertainty. We had happily dated several times, and it was clear that our togetherness was ambiguous. Yet, when we were together, we were joyfully plugged in.

I had to face myself once again with a series of questions. Had I taken a perfectly good man and turned his status into "unavailable?" Had I kissed a king and turned him into a frog? I mean, let's face it, that had been included in my list of priors. Wrecked relationship record, *oh my* ...many of my dealings traced back to the same yucky place.

Did I somehow do this to men? Did I make them unavailable? Or had they been unavailable all along? I thought it was time to take out my library of books on relationships. What did I do wrong *this* time?

I wanted a sole partner, one who turned towards me, not away. Where was he? Where was I? A dilemma, a struggle, what existed within the walls of my wretched heart? I cried out into the vastness of the universe. *Where are you, my beloved?*

I saw R2 and myself as great fit, and he did not view us in the same way. The truth lay within both of our hearts. Love is real. However, it is more functional if it is love shared by both persons.

Damn, love did it to me again!

BUB

"Believers, look up—take courage. The angels are nearer than you think."

—BILLY GRAHAM

I LUCKED OUT! I GRABBED THE BRASS RING! BUB IS ONE OF THE best guy friends I had ever known. A dear friend of mine that often took me out on boat rides called me up and had a few of his friends meet at a local bar.

Bub was intended to be a fix-up date for me. He was recently widowed from a woman he had loved for almost thirty years. He was rounding the corner on this devastatingly painful path and was ready to leave behind his sad routine, at least long enough to meet me.

Bub is very handsome, and upon our first brief encounter, I agreed to go out. He had a Paul Newman look to him, with kindness that bubbled quietly around him. Like a fountain in a Zen garden, you wanted to be near him even though you may not know exactly why.

For our first date, we met at a restaurant that overlooked crashing waves. I knew with absolute certainty that we were going to be great friends. He brought photos of his grandkids, late wife, and sailboat. I had no idea what an earth angel this gentleman would turn out to be as I sat across from him getting to know him.

A couple of days after our first date, I went over to Bub's beach condominium for a visit. As I walked up to the home, I heard the name "*Lisa*" pop into my head. As I entered his home, the name "*Lisa*" came into my thoughts two more times. Interesting, Lisa times three.

I asked him, "Bub, was your wife's name Lisa?"

He shook his head. "No, Carol."

"Strange. I keep hearing Lisa."

Bub was retired and lonely. His sense of purpose died with his wife.

I had a life-changing project ahead of me when we met. I was vacating my home of twenty-eight years and turning it into a vacation rental. It was a daunting, expensive, and tedious task that took enormous amounts of collaboration, courage, labor, imagination, and money.

Bub and I quickly became glued at the hip working at many house projects daily for months on end. We painted, shopped, and cleared cupboards. It was endless. We became very close friends by helping each other in a soulful way that went beyond mere words. The average Joe would never be able to understand the unification between us.

Some weeks after our day-to-day home improvement job, Bub met his "Lisa."

I think I was almost more excited than Bub was. She showed up and the fit seemed perfect. I did all the nudging necessary to encourage Bub on this new adventure in his life. Lisa and Bub were well-matched. Lisa had sadly lost her husband to the uninvited monster, cancer. Bub had experienced the same unthinkable sadness with his late wife, Carol. Bub had seven grandchildren and Lisa had six. They lived within two miles of one another.

It took Lisa a while to understand the soul connection Bub and I shared. It was a deep friendship and that romance was never to come of it.

Spirit definitely knows what it is speaking of. I am blessed to have an ear to hear Spirit upon occasion, and this was one of those times. Lisa was patient with Bub's job helping me finish my home project. Their love was growing daily. I was so happy that Bub's life began overflowing with love and purpose. Bub and Lisa started living together in Bub's tiny condo at the beach. They started jogging on that beach five days a week. They blended fourteen grandchildren. A very full life for Bub and Lisa.

I now occasionally spend time with these two lovebirds.

Lisa finally grabbed the brass ring, or they both did.

My Earth Angel With Boobs

"Kindred spirits are not so scarce as I used to think. It's splendid to find out there are so many of them in the world."
—L.M. Montgomery, *Anne of Green Gables*

Upon professionally photographing my home and proudly posting it online as a vacation rental, Boob Angel immediately spotted my new listing and called me. She had just sold her beach home and had to find a place for her guests that she had booked into her newly sold home. She knew the vacation rental business inside and out. Speaking with her on the phone, I could practically see the rapidly moving plates that spun in unison over her head.

"I am so grateful you are able to help me," I said to her.

"You are my angel!" I said and meant it,

"I *am* your angel! Your angel with *boobs!*" she retorted.

Hence, the birth of the name "Boob Angel."

Boob Angel came to my home in the middle of the remodel to see my vision and try to help me. A "pardon the dust, clutter, and crap" sign should have been hanging somewhere. Fresh paint extended to the unfinished sections, and my home was obviously undergoing a huge makeover.

The moment I saw her, I loved her. The connection was that

instant. She was a petite, bright, and bubbly blonde that had too many words going on all at once. This girl was adorable.

As we sat at my kitchen table, she said, "It's not fair! We were separated at birth!"

She loved me as well and was determined to help me.

Our history and lives lined up. Boob Angel had also raised her three children alone. She and her husband separated when she was carrying her third child, the same as I. Years ago, not knowing one another, we both knuckled down and became single mothers of three children. We shared much understanding, and we shared much heartache.

Boob Angel was twice the woman I was, yet half my size. She was a fireball, and I started taking notes. I could use a dose of her "kick-ass, take no prisoners" attitude. She was a confident, powerful woman that rounded things off with giggles and a glass of white wine.

We sat at my kitchen table reviewing business plans and all agreements necessary to rent out my home for short-term use. I opened up a bottle of chilled white wine and we got comfy in my kitchen and started to sip our wine. Much direction and fabulous information was fired at me via my new Boob Angel. I could not take notes fast enough.

Unaware of my behavior, I kept on snapping the blue band I had around my wrist.

Boob Angel interrupted me, then snapped, "Why in the hell do you keep doing that?"

For dramatic effect, I laid my head on the table and snapped it three more times.

"I am not taking this off until I get *laid*."

I had been "without" for far too long. It was in my bones, I was longing to be touched. I told her I was dating a great man but there was no sex. Our relationship became ambiguous and without physical attention.

I must have seemed like a girl lost without her toy. I *was* the girl lost without her toy.

"You have got to know a great guy for me?" I asked earnestly, only once.

It took less than a second for her to respond with, "Yes!"

Her best guy friend came to mind. They had been walking every morning for three years until he moved out of his home to distance himself from his wife. Boob Angel was highly organized, saucy, and intuitive. She had him call me. One minor drawback: he was still married. Dun, dun, dun . . .

My Boyfriend's A Married Man

"If I lay here. If I just lay here. Would you lie with me and just forget the world?"

—Snow Patrol

M Y BOYFRIEND'S A MARRIED MAN. NOW *THERE* IS A STATEMENT awkwardly stuttering from my lips with unrecognizable voice reflections. To be fair, (not to justify, there is *no* justification for dating a married man), he, Married Man, had filed for divorce months before we met. Or so he said.

He had been living in his own apartment for eight long and lonely months. He was sadly headed toward the end of a thirty-two-year marriage and life with someone. Or so it seemed. The dramatic change and disappointment in no manner eluded me. This was not me, until it was. I did not date married men, until I did. How did I land there?

Married Man called me and we decided to meet the next day. We met at a sidewalk café in Dana Point on a Thursday. As he was waiting for me, he eyed me upon my approach. His handsome ruggedness reminded me of Harrison Ford; six-foot-tall, weathered face, piercing blue eyes that were a bit too close, dimples to die for, and teeth that were almost too large for his smile. I caught myself staring at his hands. I loved his hands. He wore leather around his wrist, rather than a watch. His sense of style was spot on. His challenging wiry hair had just the right amount of grey on the temples and his bald spots were easily kept at bay with hairspray gracefully pulling it all together. His shoulders shrugged up to his ears, like he carried the weight of the world on them. He was six months older than me; we were both fifty-five.

Married Man was a nervous wreck. This was his first date in over thirty years. His feelings were contagious and I became nervous myself.

"I've got this," I told myself. I had first-dated so many times. I picked at my salad and chatted with him. It was pretty basic, nothing overwhelmed me with this one. I knew he was smart, I like smart, but he sounded like he was in the middle of a huge mess. My life felt much less messy.

After what was considered a pleasant lunch, he walked me to my car. Married Man placed his hand on the small of my back. Then, as dating tradition would have it, he hugged me goodbye.

It all happened in the hug. It seemed I had left my body. We both had, as we were both oddly floating over our bodies with cars zipping past us. The chemistry between us scared me. It didn't feel like sexual chemistry, it was something new to me. How could chemistry show itself in another manner?

I was bewildered. This was mysterious magic, and I was mesmerized. I drove away, not fully understanding what had just happened. The magical hug pulled me out of his mess and into his arms. I fell into him. All thoughts about his "mess" faded away. I called Boob Angel as fast as I could and expressed my excitement. Boob's matchmaking skills needed to be added to her list of talents.

I quickly renamed Married Man to "Pup" as it fit him to a tee. Whenever he had me in sight, he bounced toward me with paws too big for his body, overly enthused, and would collide right into me. He was always much too happy to see me. There was no reserve button on his feelings. He was all heart. His blue eyes bore straight through me and constantly sent me to an unfamiliar place. Pup was that guy. I quickly became the girl that eagerly sat on the curb, waiting for Pup, bracing myself just a bit.

With my home still undergoing renovations that Bub and I were working on daily, it became an ideal excuse for Pup to join us. His shiny black truck would show up as he came to help with one project after the next. Pup specialized in manufacturing one-of-a-kind items for high-end custom homes, be it gates, garage doors, and beyond, achieving the impossible for his creative clients. He was handy in all forms of construction, and helping me seemed to make him happy. Being near me seemed to make him happy.

Being near Pup made me feel all sorts of happy.

Hours of working on the house put us ready for a much-needed break. One late afternoon, we found our way to my porch swing inside my walled-in courtyard. We had worked side-by-side for hours around my home.

Bub cut out early to join his sweet Lisa. Pup and I decided to relax and swing. I felt like I was seventeen and had magically been left alone with my crush. The tenderness between us was record-breaking. I caught us gawking at one another, a game of who would blink first. His eyes shot straight through me and made something inside me turn to jelly. Without words, he then placed his hand on my heart, gently picking up my hand and placing it on his heart.

Oh, dear Lord, who does that? This moment was something out of a dime-store romance novel. A silent seduction towards love. I was toast.

Pup's feelings were so intense, and I was proud of myself for matching, or trying to match him, with an equal nonverbal message. It became a moment of powerful exchange that connected us on a level that stripped away all masks and left us both fully exposed. Trusting my feelings for this man, I had no choice but to embrace this connection. I was being swept away. The lifeguards were in sight, and I willingly sent them to rescue someone else. I swam toward Pup with an open heart, paddling as fast as I could go, trying to keep my hair dry, in place, and lip-gloss on.

I opened myself up to this powerful connection, because the pull was undeniable. To deny him would be to deny myself. This was vulnerability at its finest, for us both. We were taking a leap hand in hand.

The only thing I could look at with Pup was the present. He pulled me into it like no one ever had. He kept me planted in the moment. I knew there was risk—okay, *huge* risk—but with love, or the chance of love, I would rather take risk. Safety nets are not for me. I didn't think, I was a leap in kind of a gal. Like a fast ride at an amusement park, I waited in line and jumped on, strapping in with hopeful abandon. Sometimes reason and action come together in a direction that is scary. Hand in hand, it seemed like a leap I was willing to take. Maybe I was *that* girl after all?

We logged in numerous hours, working at my home, with intense flirting and many kisses that brought me to my knees.

Our first date was three weeks behind us.

I agreed to meet him at his apartment. I knew what that implied. I wanted to understand more about him, I needed to see and feel his space. After getting through the gate guard, my car hunted down a close parking place. I love it when my car does that. Pup was waiting with an open bottle of wine, cheese, grapes, and blueberries, setting the stage. Even though our kisses were melt-worthy, I still was unclear. I needed to be unclear. He was married. Those critical facts were simply pushed aside, and his tenderness won out.

Pup quietly asked, "Do you want to do this with me?"

Of the first steps in a relationship, being naked can be the deepest. With no assurance, I was just holding on and trusting in the nothing-ness, the everything-ness, the togetherness, the loveliness.

Happy that I had a glass of wine and grapes in my system, I whis-pered, offering up my vulnerability, "Yes, I do."

A moment, a covenant, a pact, a marriage of agreement, we were in an accord and allowed the feelings between us to be expressed in the most natural and tenderest of ways.

There had been private times in my past when I had caught my-self looking away or turning my eyes away from a lover in passionate moments. I mean, it's easy to close your eyes during sex, right? Turning into myself and focusing on feelings taking place within my body.

But with Pup, the exchange between us was beyond sexual cou-pling. With many other lovers, I went within as a self-defense mecha-nism sensing that baring my heart and soul was not safe and/or proper. Sometimes sex is just sex. Other times, it is so much more. When order-ing sex, I would rather go for the '*something more*' option. Pup offered it up with so much love and passion that it was unbelievable that we were not on our honeymoon. We couldn't keep away from one another. It was that simple. Those beautiful hands of his, if they were not on me, they were searching for me.

We sat in his dining room in our undies—actually, we were both in *his* underwear—having Chinese takeout. I paired my dining outfit with a sexy black bra. I may have been melting down, but the bra was holding up its end of the bargain. We laughed as we ate, realizing we had been in a state of nudity for several hours now, and the wine bottle was empty. Like a magnet on the fridge, our bodies found a familiar place to touch: foot, elbow, and thigh, finding their way back to their rightful nesting place. This was the true meaning of romance.

Pup was polite; he had a great deal of tender qualities. His average build was fit; he worked out five days a week. He artificially boosted his testosterone levels twice a week. I wondered if this was what made him a love machine? He had bedroom politeness, even his balls were polite. I had never known a man with polite balls until I met Pup. Oh yes, I did meet Pup's most polite balls. I was getting to know him so very well.

Clearly, I had a case of love-sickness. I knew it, because I had not known this sickness for a very long time. I had lost my appetite, and a glow was radiating from my face for the world to see. When I got near Pup, my words simply got lost. I hopelessly found myself living out moments where the best I could do was gesture and point. I would utter, "I can't talk." I was equally thrilled, over the moon, and terrified. I had to constantly remind myself to stay in the moment with Pup. Anything other than the present moment might have forced me to look at his marital status. Pup is a married man!

I found it incredulous that we would wake up at two in the morning and go after one another from the deepest parts of ourselves. I was, without a doubt, experiencing freedom and pleasure that was beyond anything I could ever remember.

The moment we became naked and vulnerable, love sickness hit me like a flu bug caught on an airplane. I began sensing that my love sickness was contagious. He followed me around like the Pup he was, waiting for his next treat. Pup viewed me as a girl who farted rainbows and pooped Twinkies. He looked at me like I was an angel. Other times he beheld me as if I was a ham sandwich and he was famished! It could only go downhill from there. Way too much reality lay in store for us. I had my share of warts as did he, it was just a matter of time until they all became exposed.

His dating skill set was unashamedly unpolished. It was charming—his wide-eyed spirit now being a part of the dating world. Refreshing in comparison to the dudes that were dating savvy and just a little bit too slick. This open-hearted Pup was all sweetness, riddled with a bit of uncertainty. Turns out, I was highly drawn to that killer combination.

However, the fact remained that Pup was currently married and worked with his wife daily. They owned a company together. He communicated face-to-face with customers and resolved the many issues people create when they have a gob of money and want something unique that has never been done. Pup and his wife's entire social network and family events happened together. There was a family gathering of some sort almost every weekend.

I was the girl that hated to be left out, but in this case I felt differently. It was his deal, and I never wanted to intrude. I easily kissed him goodbye as he went off to be with his clan.

Our relationship was planted in the now, but in the most intense and unhealthiest of ways. I willingly turned my head away from the woeful reality. I turned my eyes toward him, his eyes were on me, it was all just a series of moments that strung themselves together within the walls my heart. I forced myself to never look into the future for fear that I would strap on my running shoes, running away in search of safety.

This relationship would soon be jam-packed with the great challenges ahead of us, or, mostly in front of him. Real issues existed, like a shoreline you can never quite see that is shrouded by the unknown.

Pup never called me from his cell phone because Wife paid the bills and checked in on what he was up to. I felt awful for her, but not awful enough. I knew that feeling of sickening distrust as she analyzed Pup's phone bills all too well. It made me feel ill to my stomach. He only contacted me through email or calls made from his home phone. I was aware of how bad this whole story sounded. Clearly it was bad. I agree. It was deplorable. I was deplorable.

I found myself on the other end of the "other woman" scenario, and it sucked on every other level. Was this irony or catharsis? I wasn't sure. l did not want to be the "other woman." I swore I would never be the "other woman." I was simply not wired that way. The utter essence of me screamed, "I am '*THE* woman,' not the '*THE* other woman!'"

Yet here I was, "other-woman-ing" it. How in the hell did I let this happen? This meant I was not really the significant part of my sweetheart's life. However, I didn't feel like the "rebound girl" or "the other woman." It felt more like Pup was in transition, finding his way, when in fact, I also was in transition, finding my own way.

We related deeply to one another, and our connection was undeniably powerful. This was what it was, so I still casually dated other men. There was no reason not to. As often as he ran off to family gatherings, I simply refused to be the girl who sat idle and waited for his return. Other than the ridiculous fact that my heart spoke a language for him and him only. Shit.

Then again, there was R2. I wasn't perfectly ready to let go of that possibility, of *our* possibility. I had two semi-boyfriends at 55, and I refused to judge myself for this. Is it quite possible that they were, boy oh boy, two half boyfriends? Was I here once again? This hadn't worked the first time around. Was I crazy? Big and Exception led to *exceptionally big* disappointments. If combined, would I really have one whole boyfriend? I was dumbfounded.

I told R2 that I was not exactly twiddling my thumbs during our *ambiguous* dating status, and I was, in fact, dating outside of our unpredictable schedule. I just hadn't copped the business details to my Pup.

I thought he would feel crushed.

I knew I would, a double standard of feelings. Suddenly, I was glad I would be in Oregon for two weeks. My girlfriend Pooh, happily nick-named by her sassy grandchildren, lived in Eugene, and I was going to combine a trip and housesit for her as well. R2 was going to drive me to the airport since Pup would have had to explain himself to his wife. Half dating a married man sucked!

Although I found myself befuddled in this duel love scenario, I was well aware these two men were far closer and more loving than any one man I had known in years. Maybe I *was* doing better?

IRONY, IRONY

"Never say goodbye, because goodbye means going away and going away means forgetting."
—J.M. BARRIE'S *PETER PAN*

I RONY: NO ONE CAN AVOID IT. I THINK WE CREATE IT.
During the summer, I was looking forward to being in Oregon for a few weeks, staying along the Mackenzie River in Eugene. I planned on hanging out with one of my best gal pals, Pooh, and her manly-man husband, who she endearingly called Luvie. It had been six months since I'd last seen her, so we were both extremely excited to reunite.

Pooh is my daughter's mother-in-law. Pooh and I also happen to be soul sisters that can party until the sun comes up. She's such a babe, with the ability to deliver any kind of news with the sweetest tone and smile. You can even find yourself thanking her for handing you day old eggs. Somehow those eggs were exactly what you wanted. That girl is a clever one. I readily took notes in awe of her.

Since Tiburon was on the way to Eugene, I considered driving and stopping by to see Lover. I knew it might not be my smartest move, seeing how I felt about Pup. But Lover and I were in the friend zone, so it shouldn't be weird, right? I mean, I *loved* Tiburon.

How unexpected that when I decided to text Lover about my idea, he said he actually wasn't in Tiburon anymore. No, *uh huh*, he was in

Eugene, reunited with his ex-girlfriend. I better book fight arrangements.

Hmmm. Well, at least that visit was out of the question.

I adored Pooh's home. It was altogether peaceful and sweet, filled with two dogs, an inside cat, and a barn kitty, Miss Elle, who hissed at me when I walked up to the attic to greet her. Picturesque views could be witnessed from every window in their two-story English country home. The driveway was so long that I enjoyed riding her bike up to grab the mail from the street. The house was in a perfect country setting, with pink blossomed trees lining the road and deer constantly frolicking about. There were white lined fences and pastures of grazing horses surrounding the property that bordered the McKenzie river.

A few days into my Oregon visit, Lover texted me. He wanted to see me, seeing as I was in the same town as him and all. It was fate that we landed in the same place, right? Everything happens for a reason, so I had to see him. I wanted to see him. My life was complicated enough with Pup and R2. It was way too easy to throw an ex-Lover into the mix. Was I stirring things up for a reason? Maybe.

Lover drove over to the English country home in his familiar Mercedes puppy van. I half-expected to see his new/old girlfriend walk out of the car with him, and I was relieved when she didn't appear. Like a kid with an old/new toy, I didn't want to share. That statement alone was ridiculous seeing how I willingly shared Pup with his wife. Oh well.

As he hopped out of his canine kennel (on chrome wheels), we just stared at each other and laughed. How crazy was this adventure we called life—we met in Newport Beach, Corona Del Mar, the fanciest of beach towns, then Rancho Santa Fe, then Tiburon, and here we were, in the rain forest of Oregon's countryside. A long way from home, and still we ended up at the same place. I love fate.

We embraced for a long, welcoming hug, and the familiar response to his body pressed against mine went straight to my knees, uninvited. When had we been naked together last? Oh, that's right, Tiburon. In this moment, it seemed like just yesterday.

He stood before me in full Lover fashion, and I could only think about how amazing he looked, how amazing he'd always looked. Damn, he had just showered and smelled like mossy lavender.

Internally I told myself, "I cannot fool around with him, I have two half boyfriends!" I repeated this to overcome my Lover weakness. How could I turn that into a mantra? I was pretty sure all mantras excluded anything to do with half boyfriends.

We jumped into Luvie's Mini Cooper and roared into town for lunch. Lover was always nuts behind the wheel, and I laughed at his speeding outbursts.

"Do not go down the driveway at this speed, there are deer!"

Scolding him like a wife felt *way* too good. He slammed on his brakes because, of course, on cue, out popped Bambi, frolicking down the long driveway.

"See, I told you!"

We laughed at the timing of it all. We were having fun.

Pooh, being a betting gal, had put fifty dollars down on us having sex during our encounter. I was glad to know she believed in Lover's— or my—ability, or lack of ability, to "keep it in the pants."

Lunch was sweet and the fun progressed over margaritas. He wanted to do some shopping, so we went to Old Navy where he bought jeans on sale for $18.50. How was it that people with deep pockets still loved a deal? As he was trying them on, I was peeking in—no need to feel badly about that. He also picked up some socks for me that I eventually forgot about. They made their way back home with him, and I am sure his girlfriend appreciated the thoughtful gift, *my* socks. She got the socks and the guy. Oh, and the pillow from Tiburon.

I didn't hate her, I swear.

I asked Lover if he would like me to show him around the mall, and he said, "Sure . . . this is just about spending time with you."

His momentary kindness struck me. I had never quite figured out what was the deal between Lover and me. I may just die wondering.

Was he a tongue in my thighs or a thorn in my side? Easily both.

We headed back to my temporary country home and decided to walk about the property. I was trying to extend our time together. Afterword, we sat under the rose-lined arbor and took in the moment. Feeling the proximity of our bodies, the perfect summer day, and the familiar draw, Lover must have read my mind.

Lover looked right into my eyes and said, "If I had sex with you, you would not respect me."

Sitting wide-eyed in silence, I had nothing to say to that. I felt momentary disappointment. I wanted to feel the closeness that we knew, a closeness that was always good.

Just like our welcome hug, our goodbye hug lasted a long while. Had we been naked, it would have been sex right there in the garden, amongst the deer...

He left and called me three minutes later. The way he drove, it must have been three miles out.

"*Hey*, I just wanted you to know I felt bad about leaving . . . I almost turned around at the end of the driveway. I could have at least been neighborly and gone *down* on you."

I paused at this unexpected glimmering possibility, the angel on one shoulder and the devil on the other. Again, Lover struck me down to silence. My jaw dropped and no words came out.

Oh my, how thoughtful! Had Lover become more neighborly? Wow, they didn't have neighbors like that where I came from! One more reason to move, check. Real neighborly folks, these transplanted Oregonians. Go Ducks!

I had to excuse myself and get the ending he had suggested for me. I very soon realized he was right, that I would not have respected him had he assisted me on this momentary venture. He was currently living with his girlfriend. Interesting that I respected that, but turned a blind eye with Pup.

Pooh lost her bet. We did not have sex. We thought about it, but we did not. Or we thought about *presidential sex*—is that what they were calling oral sex now? I don't care what anyone says, it is still sex!

Nomad In Heels

"Life is an adventure, it's not a package tour."
—Eckhart Tolle

I STOOD AT MY FRONT DOOR WITH MY WORLD PACKED UP AT MY feet. Lugging my entire life with me, I literally had baggage in my possession. My home was finally a vacation rental, and it was officially time for me to go.

I grabbed my pink overnight bag and stuffed it full of outfit possibilities as I got ready for my next sleepover. Something about my small, plastic-lined shopping bag brought me serious comfort, grasping for familiarity within my changes.

Was it weird that I could fit my current life into the trunk of my car? Wait, did I have enough underwear options? Okay, three extra pairs just for good measure. *Oh!* I almost forgot my Batman ones! I needed my favorite pink cotton Batman underwear to sleep in. This time, I had to spend a week away from my home. I had to remind myself every one of those days away that this was my job, this was my income. I found much gratitude in my wandering, as I pushed away trepidation.

Amongst other things in my life, I had made an art out of packing. It took me about fifteen minutes to stuff my necessities into a to-go bag and hit the road. Some men made my nomadic life easier. They would buy me items that I usually, and often, overlooked in my own home. Towels, pillows, blankets, shampoo, contact solution, anything I could call my "own" in their space. Okay, one less thing to pack, thank you. These kind gestures did not escape me.

Oh, if I was given "the drawer," I was feeling better about my guy and myself. It was a very welcoming feeling having my comforting contents await me upon my return visit.

One time, Big politely handed me a small bag of "my things" the morning after one of our nightly endeavors. This gesture sent a strong message: "You're just a guest, take your belongings as you head towards the exit, which is located on your left. Thank you for your visit, and when invited, please, do come again." The funniest thing about that bag was the fact that it held contents from a previous "guest." Big was the type of man who allowed all levels of intimacy but would not allow my generic contact solution in his bathroom built for two. Big joke. Big's covert behavior was loud and clear, which made it easier to leave and even more difficult to return. I was welcomed only upon demand.

On that particular week long hiatus from my home, I kept thinking about the pillow Lover got me in Tiburon, a short-lived gesture. The material things guys buy to welcome women into their homes were sometimes confusing.

Had he done this with other girls? Was I the first one to get my own pillow? Of course not all guys welcome girls into their homes and lives, but there's something vulnerable about them when they do. Little things make me feel like I am permanent, or, at least important in that moment, it really feels good. A glisten in a man's eye tells me they are thrilled to spend the extra money in order to make me feel at home in their personal kingdom. I was forever testing, on some level, if I was worthy of being their Queen.

Truth is, I was Goldilocks. Always fleeing in search of my next pillow, because the one before it was not "just right." When would I land on the bed that would be "my," no, "our" permanent bed? Who knew? Time would tell. I may just have to get adjusted to different sheets; let's hope they have a high thread count. Perhaps it was time to take myself pillow shopping. Just like Goldilocks, I was looking for that "one" perfect bed.

Too Soon For Goodbye

"I'm late, I'm late, for a very important date! No time to say hello, goodbye! I'm late, I'm late, I'm late!"

—Lewis Carroll's *Alice In Wonderland*,
The White Rabbit

I ENJOYED A LONG, SUN-FILLED DAY IN THE HARBOR WITH BUB AND Pup. A live band was rocking out at the end of the dock to kick off the summer. It was Memorial Day weekend, so Bub, Pup, and I took Bub's dinghy out for a putz around the waterways.

I was quickly dubbed the "curly-haired captain of the dinghy." I felt an odd sense of power behind the wheel. It was as if I had the world on a string. Lulling about the salty, briny sea, I could not be more thrilled. I was with my two handsome guys. Laughing, drinking beers, this side of wonderful filled me with utter happiness. I was ideally living inside a sunscreen or Viagra commercial, minus the hair and makeup. It was perfection on a summer day.

The affection and heartfelt connection I felt with Pup was alive and well. We couldn't keep our hands off of each other. Pup gave me neck and head massages whenever he had the chance. I leaned in to kiss him every moment that presented itself.

Pup had my phone in his hand, politely holding on so it did not fall into the harbor water. Along came a couple of ill-timed texts. R2 was checking on my weekend plans.

Sitting at the front of Bub's sailboat, as we watched other boats pass by, I squared off with Pup. Knee to knee and eye to eye, it was time for honesty. The waters were calm as we sat in the shade.

Was I going to leave the elephant in the room? That wouldn't work. We were on a boat, and we'd capsize for sure.

Looking Pup in the eye, I blurted out, "I am dating other men!"

He sat silent with a pretty good poker face.

I continued, "You are not available to me now. I would like it to be different . . . but I don't see a change with you, so this is what I am doing."

My forthrightness was refreshing to him, and he told me how "grown-up" I was.

With Pup, looking intensely into each other's eyes seemed to be our thing. It shot straight into my soul with skilled accuracy. He may have been Robin Hood in his past life. Those stares were awakening my heart, bit by bit. Tearing me apart, brick by brick, breaking down the walls that carefully protected my heart. His kind stillness somehow cut deeper into me than anything ever had.

Pup told me that he had started to write me an email. I imagined a "Dear John" type letter emerging from his fingertips. His intentions were clear and stated that he did not want to pull me into his sandstorm, where snakes were biting at his ankles.

As I started to understand, my heart sank to the bottom of the harbor and beyond. I was thinking, "I'm okay with snakes and sand. Let's go at it together, 'Team Sandstorm!'"

Suddenly, I felt sick to my stomach. I had to come to terms with the fact that this was his journey, and how he got through it was solely up to him. As a girlfriend, I was required to respect that. It seemed as though I was grown-up after all.

Pup said, "It isn't responsible for us to continue seeing one another."

"We need to say goodbye?" I said it like it was a question. It was in no way a question.

After our breakup conversation, we made our way to the back of the boat. The space was tiny, yet familiar. We were lying in the v-berth, wrapped in each other's arms fully clothed, intertwining legs, bodies, and tears. Both of us seemed torn up about having to "say goodbye." With salt in the air and on our cheeks and our noses running, it was quite the scene. I knew that Pup and I had no causal connection where we could just become buddies. I began to feel my heart shatter piece by piece, moment by moment.

In order to break the silence and continue what we had started at the bow of the boat, I said, "You're right, we need to say goodbye."

I couldn't believe that we were ending our relationship. My spirit knew, with great certainty, that it was much too soon to shut down this unification. Pup was protecting himself and protecting me as well in the process.

I changed my mind quickly and told him, "It is too soon for us to part. It is too soon to say goodbye."

I knew he heard me, but I said, again, "It is too soon to say good-bye."

I felt that all the way through my soul. We were not supposed to be done yet. It was just too soon.

"What you felt, I felt," he responded.

Those words were as much as he could manage, and I knew it.

I realized I was not alone in my feelings, and that fact somehow helped me cope with my seasick emotions. I realized this was the end. I may never see this man again, so this was my only chance.

Looking into Pup's eyes, the place I once found great comfort in, I announced, "I love you."

I honestly proclaimed it thinking that this was my last chance to see him, the last chance to tell him. A raw truth submerged from my heart. I was proud of myself for being real, for speaking my truth. There was no way I was going to show anything but naked honesty in that moment.

After all, this was my naked journey, and raw truth was my new armor. It was an outfit I had to trust. When love presents itself, truth must be real, and it was real. This all came as no surprise to Pup. That might have been part of the problem: this was not a casual see-ya-later deal, and we both knew that.

We had to say goodbye. Goodbye is what had to be done. Easy, right? Done and done. Dropping Pup off at his doorstep took over an hour. He did not want to leave my car. I wanted him to invite me in. It was torture at its finest.

Finally parting ways, I made it back to the harbor to pick up Bub and collapse in a raw sob scene. Bub was in shock. I was a basket case. Bub and I knew tears, so this was an easy, yet painful, moment for both of us. What a pair we were.

It had been a long day filled with sun and salty air. Well after midnight, we were both tired, so we made our way back to Bub's home. His sweet Lisa was out of town, and, seeing how I was a broken-hearted, homeless, curly-haired captain of the dinghy, I took the bed. Bub slept on the couch. I loved Bub, and this night was full of love as well as heartache.

Providence Had Its Way

"There is a fine line between serendipity and stalking."

—David Coleman

IF YOU BELIEVE IN FORCES OF NATURE, GOD, SPIRIT, THE GREAT Divine, as I do, you don't mess with said faith.

Waking up, Bub says to me, "Girl, I'm still shocked over Pup."

Bub and I cried in our coffee. We knew how to cry together. He was a friend for laughter, and a friend for tears.

Later that morning, Bub popped back over to the boat to meet with his daughter and granddaughter. I decided to write, bathe, and try to shake off the feeling that Pup and I had not to come to our end quite yet, even though we had said goodbye the night before. It just didn't feel right.

After hours of weeping, heartache, writing, and coffee, I was famished, so my first stop was the local deli to order myself a "grief sandwich." It was delivered in the form of an egg salad sandwich. With my arms loaded with goodies for Bub's boat, I stepped out of the deli.

I stopped dead in my tracks, and my jaw dropped. Scene one: the camera panned to the conflicted, freshly showered, and somewhat tired-looking man who stepped out of a shiny black truck. The one, the only, the heartbreaker Pup, was standing smack dab in front of me. Uh, wow. This town was not *that* small. After a moment of being entrenched in the serendipitous moment, Pup suggested we have our sandwiches together… Uh, *yeah.*

Pup had given me the chance to say everything that I had needed to say last night. That included, but was not limited to, the "I love you" that spilled from my painfully honest lips. I found myself suddenly regretting my exposed feelings. Damn, shit, crap, hells bells, fudge bucket, why had I been so forthright? Oh, that's right, it's *my* honest naked journey! Ugh.

We sat quietly on an empty patio adjacent to the deli parking lot. So, with little left to say, I sat on his lap. It seemed like the right thing to do at the moment. Pup agreed to help me with outdoor lighting that needed to be replaced in my vacation rental home and spoke of a key that was under his mat waiting for me. Pup had officially presented me with an "outdoor key" to his apartment.

I thanked him and asked him to keep the key there for the time being.

He said, "Deal."

I've learned to listen to Spirit. Now, Spirit's message was clear; "It was too soon for goodbye." Spirit had put this message on my heart, saying, "Here you go, you two figure it out."

As relationships change and undefined lines become defined, things can shift or slide a bit backward. Pup and I decided to keep our moments together in private. He was in a fragile situation, and I was accepting him on less than ideal terms. *Okay*, on really less than ideal terms. I was giving him time, as I knew he needed. Ending three decades of a life could be severely altering. As lovely and appealing as Pup was, it was increasingly obvious that I felt uncomfortable with this situation. Moreover, it put me in the position to date others outside of Pup's closed doors, and I would. I could only imagine how hard this was for Pup. This was our reality and we only existed behind closed doors.

R2 And Billy

"I'd rather laugh with the sinners than cry with
the saints—the sinners are much more fun."
—Billy Joel

O NE NIGHT, R2 AND I WENT OFF TO A BILLY JOEL CONCERT TO
sit in box seats, seventh row center. I was *very* excited to see Billy
and spend a fun night with R2. I deeply understood that a square peg
and round hole would always have their challenges.

We agreed, ahead of time, that I would spend the night after the
concert. I was currently homeless, as my home was in vacation rental
mode.

To leave my house of three decades and set off into the unknown
had proven to be a life-changing transition. I was like a gypsy, jumping
into the abyss with a smile on my face while trembling on the inside.
I was living out of my expensive car, going from friend to friend each
night, finding my way to a bathroom that was not the same one I had
used the night before. Where the hell was the light switch? I hated to
flush in the middle of the night and wake up the household, but it was
either that or running the risk of leaving pee in the toilet. Damn, what
home was I in now? Should I flush or not flush?

R2 and I hopped into his well-appointed Mercedes Benz with
hours to spare before the concert, knowing we had to battle our way

through the famous rush hour Los Angeles traffic. He proceeded to talk about his work and how much it had evolved and flourished. Much of the intimate conversation came very unexpectedly. R2 was setting out to open only one clinic and by happenstance and divine intervention, there would be seven total. R2 was intent on explaining his purpose and his life's design. He explained that he wanted to have someone by his side to enjoy all that he had worked so hard for. He was a King that had built a kingdom to bring in a Queen and "all that that implied." This included travel, private planes, and a willingness to "take care of someone." This was a well thought out message he decided to deliver to me. I slowly realized that R2's future talk had been designed and measured with *me* in mind.

I was starting to see that this was some kind of proposal. R2 was sweetly lacking in obvious romance and awkwardly leaning toward a PowerPoint presentation. I gave him grace. This was who he was and how he managed his thoughts and emotions. I listened with great intent. My heart began to swell as I connected the dots on the spot. He had been pushing me away for so long. How could this be? I was stunned. He continued describing his life and how he wanted to share it with someone.

This all came at me sideways; I was utterly bewildered. With a somewhat incredulous tone, I finally asked, "Do you think I'm *your* person?"

He simply answered, without hesitation, "Yes, I think you're *my* person."

Did I just stop breathing? I think I did.

My mind was racing really fast yet painfully slow at the same time. So many things were running through my head. They all collided into garbled, nonsensical clutter. Okay, this fuzzy picture was beginning to get clearer.

"I'm going to need to process this. Please give me a couple of days. I will probably have some questions for you," I finally responded. I sweetly put my hand on his arm and left it there for a long while. Physical affection is one of my strongest love languages. I was showing him love.

The irony here was timing. He had been my person, but that was many weeks ago, or was it months ago? All I knew was that it felt like centuries ago now. Timing was an unfair, cruel, fickle bitch, at least, our timing seemed to be. Did they say "fickle bitch" centuries ago? I had a heart for R2, his cause, and his soulful purpose in life.

I marveled with a curious heart, "Is this where I am meant to be?" By this man's side, being taken care of, well and safe … laughing my days into the future?

I asked myself the real question. "Does he love me?" If he did, would I have to ask? Shouldn't I already know? I got lost in a whirlpool of obsession and contemplation. That familiar place that sends me into a series of questions, one right after the next, leaving no thought unturned, and finally sending me off into exhaustion coupled with utter anguish.

Where could I possibly fit in R2's PowerPoint presentation proposal? I did not hear him say anything about my remarkable charming self. My second love language is words.

Note to self: ask him, "What is it about me that makes you feel I'm your person?"

Two weeks later, I asked just that at our favorite sushi place. After the proper amount of unfiltered sake, which resembled mother's milk, with a kick equal a heavy prescription medication delivered intravenously, I mustered up the courage to have that conversation.

I asked R2, "Why do you think I'm your person, the one who you want to place beside yourself in your future?"

He answered with ease, "I liked the way your hair goes in twelve different directions, and you don't care. You can, and have, run out of the house with your t-shirt on backwards. Looks don't matter after you're old as salt, no one cares, and you don't now. You have a wide-eyed love for people all around you. But your heart, your heart is good, you don't have a mean bone in your body."

He saw a certain sweetness in me, I could feel it. I am impulsive, and my mouth can fly open unpredictably. R2 was okay with that. I dance in public when a good song hits my ears. I can be reckless at times, and he is the one to see me to safety. He protected me like a real man does. I smile and say hello to most people like we are long lost friends, and R2 always stood anchored by my side. I saw myself as a handful. He saw me as his.

I understood him, and this talk helped me to process and accept his gesture for what it was: a gesture. I never needed to answer. As much as I had great love and respect for R2, we were not the right fit. Our love languages did not match.

R2's follow through with me lately had been inconsistent and lame. How busy could a person be? No one is too busy for a brief call or text. I was guessing that, after he presented a lifelong offer to me and I didn't jump out of my seat, he might be backing off. I had not gotten the kind of attention I needed from R2 for a long while. I decided I would wait for him to come around with a patient heart. Anything less would be short-changing us both. Spirit had told me loud and clear, "Be patient." I had to listen to Spirit versus any nagging, naysaying thoughts. That could build up like plaque in the long run.

I was well aware of the fact that R2 and his promises were more than most people could ever hope for in a lifetime. I had such great affection for him and found utter joy in our time together. We found laughter in simply lying in bed together and finding each other. R2's thoughts came together in a weird, quirky, and hilarious way. He always surprised me with his humorous view on life. Smiling in his arms was always a safe and happy place to be.

And when the doors were closed, and the party was over, forget it, he was sweet then too.

The question would then have to be, "Is there a home for me in his heart? Or is there a home for him in my heart?"

I was not sure if R2 was in love with me. Yet didn't he have to be in love with me if he offered his future to me? Bottom lines can be hard sometimes. Was that the bottom line, love? To love or not to love, *ah*, that was the question! If I had to question if R2 loved me, or if I loved him, I already had the answer. I hate Shakespeare; that dude figured it out long before I got here.

R2 may not have had enough motivation to be attentive to me. That was the sad truth, so I sat and waited. When the moment presented itself, I would be as honest as I could and let him know what it would take to make me happy. I just had to give it time. It felt like some kind of fogged-in day at the San Francisco airport, just waiting for the clouds to lift. Passengers crowded in the terminal, waiting, pacing, just trying to kill the time because they were headed somewhere else. I felt as if I were waiting amongst them, not alone, just another number. I closed my eyes, wondering if there was a blue sky somewhere. Was I just waiting to be somewhere else?

Boob Angel always said actions speak louder than words. It was getting pretty quiet in the fog waiting for R2 to roll around.

Two Minus Two Equals Zero

"I only like two kinds of men, domestic and imported."

—Mae West

WITH TWO HALF BOYFRIENDS, IT GOT A BIT TRICKY WITH THE scheduling. This dual dating situation, of course, offered up perks as well as complications. I had the guy to take me to all the fancy-schmancy events in public, and I had the other guy who wanted to sleep next to me and touch me at all times, but only in private. I rode out this dual dating situation far too easily and far too long.

I understood that I was much closer to what I wanted, as these men were kind, loving, and filled my list unlike before. I had found a boyfriend for every purpose. I reasoned out that neither guy was willing to claim an exclusive relationship with me. My only complaint was that neither of them were "*all in.*" Well, the joke was on me, because neither was I! I had two men. How, or why, would I be all in with one?

Although I very much loved both R2 and Pup, I found myself griping about the situation I had created. No one else I knew at the time went out and got themselves two half boyfriends. The one thing my two boyfriends had in common was me. This was no one's fault but mine.

I let R2 off the hook and allowed him to reach out to me on his schedule and at his whim. It made perfect sense at the time. It began to feel as though he was taking advantage of this option, as he began exercising his full rights to minimal contact. I had to be honest, I wanted, needed, and required more. As women, society tells us to never nag about getting too little care. This will lead men into thinking they are dealing with their nagging mothers, in which case they will shut down and turn into the three-year-olds they once were. I was done parenting, I was looking for a different gig.

With Pup, well, I willingly jumped in knowing he was in the middle of the sandstorm. Wanting a married man was like being hungry, desperate, outdoors, wandering in the desert, and waiting for roadkill. There was no one to blame but myself. I wanted a man that was available for only me, yet I was not really available for either of those lovely men that were loving me.

Oh, the dreaded repeated breakups. Pup and I went to go break up for the third time, or was it the fourth? After our first boat breakup, we attempted many different ways to part. None of them worked. I may have lost count in our crazy breakup pattern. Each time I had the same reaction as the first, gut-wrenching agony. Either Wife or I would have to get over Pup, and I was pretty sure it was going to have to be me. Each time we broke up felt like the last time. I would run to the toilet and find myself getting sick from one end or the other. How many times would I have to experience this before I realized that this was an unhealthy cycle for me?

Wait! Maybe Pup was right, perhaps it was time to put on my big girl panties and be one hundred percent available for a man that was all in for me. I hated the fact that my boyfriends were both only half in, but so was I! As the juggling lady, I needed to take half the blame. I had to sweep up my side of the street and have a serious talk with both of my boyfriends. At separate times, of course. My head would blow up if they were both sitting together. Too many condemning, raised eyebrows accompanied that vision.

I would have a face-to-face sit down with the two half boyfriends. I was without a home, and, soon, I would be without my guys. If I wanted a man to be solely focused on me, then I would have to become the same. Although I had some big fun having two half boyfriends, that Shakespearean play would no longer work for me.

Breaking Up Is Hard To Do

"Whether you're throwing up or breaking up, you want your girlfriend right there! I don't trust women who don't go to their girlfriends."
—DREW BARRYMORE

BREAKUPS WERE APPARENTLY MUCH HARDER THAN I THOUGHT . . . I knew it was in my best interest to discontinue this scenario. I imagined myself becoming untethered, finally getting both feet on the ground. I wanted to be all in with one guy. That was my unending goal. Having a boyfriend for every purpose was part of my expedition, but my goal had always been one real love, one man for all purposes. Yet there I was, neatly justified between two men. Justified but questioning.

With Pup, tremendous effort and conversation always lead us back to the same place, a place of no change. Either that, or said change was indeed going at a snail's pace. We'd come back together with comforting familiarity; it was crazy in the making. The sex was unbelievable. I could hardly keep up with it. Was Pup trying to work the sex out of me? Claiming sexual ownership, planting one's flag? Our chemistry went far beyond sex. We were so entwined that we morphed into one body while we slept together. We woke up one morning to one of my feet and one of his feet together in his underwear leg. Like a three-legged race, but racing to no end. We blissfully slept in this cotton concoction without knowledge of the fact that we were bound up. Who did that? Uh, Pup and I did.

I may have needed to move at this point, but I wasn't sure that would be enough. Maybe to a foreign country? Clearly, I was not ready to throw in the towel, the sheets, or the shared underwear tourniquet with Pup. He was my comfort zone, my bubble bath, my security blanket. He made my heart swell. I know, *gag*. Wasn't he supposed to be the summer fling? Crap!

I was thinking that breaking up would go much smoother with R2, and we would easily part. He would probably be relieved, and we, of course, would remain dear friends. I had to stop trying to control these outcomes.

I waited a couple of weeks to see R2 and figured we could chat then. He announced he had gotten us fifth row, center seats to see Santana.

R2 told me, "Life was hard this week, and we both need a distraction." There comes the devil on one shoulder and the angel on the other. I wanted my cake and I wanted to eat it too. I cared too much for R2 not to share with him how I was feeling.

I went to R2's home and let him know all I needed was a friendship and that any romantic ties would not work for me at this time. He was upset. Giving him, and myself, grace, I headed home, on a sad drive filled with reasonable doubt and definite disappointment. Fragmented relationships no longer served me. He called me a couple of hours after I got home.

R2 said, "Well, we have the concert to go to."

I replied, "Yes, we do!" If I could have jumped into his arms over the phone, I would have. "But," I stammered, "Is it okay that we are friends?"

It was too soon. Maybe he felt it long before our conversation? R2 was a smart man.

He reassured me, "It is okay that we are friends."

Even with the shift that *finally* made our relationship status clear as "friends," I knew we would still have a blast at the concert.

Unraveling At The Seams

"It's not the load that breaks you down, it's the
way you carry it."

—Lou Holtz

ANXIETY ROSE UPON ME QUICKLY. I FOUND MYSELF HEADING FOR
a temporary, but very real, nervous breakdown.

I was talking to Healer on the phone, and, with the sweetest voice,
she said, "You don't sound like yourself, are you okay?"

Her tender words were enough for me to split in two. I started
crying. I could not find my breath. Breathing was the one thing that
was constant and stable. Where was my breath? The hiccups returned
for the first time in many years. I saw myself, small and standing in
my childhood hallway. How long had I been fighting with that private
demon? It was altogether much too familiar. Hiccups squeaked in my
ears. I felt out of my body and sick to my stomach at the same time.
This transition became too much for me to handle.

Breaking up with R2 and feebly trying to break up with Pup within
days of each other, coupled with living in different homes every week,
was really taking a toll on me. Never mind the different home part. It
turned out I was becoming unglued not knowing how to dial in the
"just right" bath in other people's bathtubs; it must have been the Goldilocks in me. After all, hot baths were where I could float in peace, alone

from all the outside noise. Baths had always been my place for comfort.

I took a turn for the worst and was circling the drain. I could not see past dread and missing breaths. Where had my once stable breathing gone? I was clearly lacking the security associated with my home and the continuity that once bred comfort within me. I somehow became lost. I was in some kind of continuous pain. The thing with pain is that it always appears for a reason. Pain shows up in full force to tell me something. I just didn't understand what the reason or message was this time around. *Please help me pain, you are so loud.*

I was melting down and found myself unable to function. I had to get home. Ha! I had no home, my home was full of high-paying renters. I had to get back to where my suitcase was, where my traveling world was, my pink bag, and just stay put.

I was dog-sitting for a new friend. However, I was in no shape to get behind the wheel. In a haze, I drove through the gates, gave my paper pass to the shaved-headed, mindless gate guard, and finally got to my temporary dwelling.

"Please let me get to my temporary pink bag full of unnecessary items to make me feel sane again," I thought. I needed to feel sane.

Pup came to the rescue with lunch and love. He ran off to the drugstore to pick up some calm-down-now medicine and various needed items. My wonderful doctor gave grace to my temporary state of bat-shit crazy. My darling Pup, who I wanted to break from, *ha*, stayed with me even when I was not myself.

My new friend, who happened to be gay, was living in a sweet home by the beach. I was beginning to cherish the new friendship with my gay friend. I would never have to break up with this man, and that was comforting. Oh, that's right, breaking up was on my to-do list. It was an unsuccessful goal that I had only half accomplished.

I was a balloon lost in a sky of sorrow. Pup was planted on the ground holding onto the string, not letting me drift too far away. He saw that I ate, like a mother bird. Then he dragged me down to the beach after sunset, with a vintage wool blanket in hand. The sky was turning a color that goes beyond description. We lay down without words and stared up at the heavens. I was silent. I was numb. The waves were making all the noise that I needed to hear. The rhythm of the surf started to lull me. I was still struggling to reach beyond my pain as the infinite sprawled before us in the stars. Pup rested a hand on me and started to breathe deep and slow. Salt air filled my lungs as my breathing slowed in order to match his. Isn't that what we did? Breathe together. Without effort, my breath found his. I hated that we were this connected. I loved that we were this connected.

Pup's tenderness gave me permission to feel what I had to feel and be all right with that. He was a man that wanted to, and consistently did, take care of me. He quietly lay next to me. I was on my own, in my own world, but I knew he was somewhere nearby. The sounds of the surf and the expansiveness of the sky were perfection. I needed to cry. I didn't know why, but I did. Although tears did not come to me that night, a hidden peace may have.

It took me three very long days to come out of my anxious funk. It was no fun forgetting all my blessings, feeling so small, and having difficulty finding my breath. Pup saw me through this time, and I was grateful for that. I returned to myself after being lost in a vacant and sad space. Three days of silence, three days of curling within and looming darkness. My heart went out to those who suffer in the darkness and do not pull out within seventy-two hours like I mercifully did.

Darkness is darkness.

My Married Boyfriend And The Outdoor Key

"Being insecure—I'm a master, a virtuoso—they can be handing me the keys to the kingdom and all I can think is, I hope I don't drop the key."
—M. Night Shyamalan

WHAT WAS I SUPPOSED TO MAKE OF BEING GIVEN ACCESS TO AN outdoor key by my married boyfriend? This key under a mat was left by Pup for me to use at any point in time. Seeing how I was a Goldilocks-ish nomadic gypsy at the time, Pup's gesture was, indeed, welcomed. I mean, my choices of homes were Bub's boat, with limited bathroom usage, or mustering up the courage to flip over a "welcome" mat and use "my" designated key. What did it mean that Pup offered me his hidden house key? This could be a big deal for some men. It could mean he was offering up keys to his kingdom.

If I had learned one thing throughout this expedition, it was that guys are not as complicated as I thought. Maybe I am, or the female species are, the ones who make things all a jumble? From what I can see, guys are simple and want to make us gals happy. The language and meaning between the sexes gets so quickly convoluted that it astonishes me. For example, I was stumped at the offering of the key.

Okay, so which guy could explain to me what the outdoor key from Pup meant? Was the gallant offering of the house key a sign of love, trust, what? It did not escape me that he was allowing me into his domestic empire.

It's one thing to be handed a set of house keys, but another to be presented with the outdoor key option, or a garage code for that matter. How had I earned this outdoor option? It must have been my Batman undies, *duh*.

Perhaps unraveling this mystery was not as important as finding a cozy place to stay for the night?

With Pup, I had advanced to a clicker for the gate and a garage code. Bub had handed me a fob to park in the private boat parking lot, a key to get past the gated docks, and a skeleton key to enter the boat. I could not read further into any of this, because I would get nowhere in my assumptions. All I knew was that I was welcomed at several different places, and I was very grateful for it.

Hell In A Handbasket

"Go to Heaven for the climate, Hell for the company."

—Mark Twain

Boob Angel and I went out for breakfast on a beautiful summer morning. I had just returned from a much-welcomed extended stay in Oregon, seeing my Boob Angel was in order. She was renting out my home for the entire month of August alongside her adoring husband and two English sheepdogs.

We headed down to the harbor to her favorite spot. She breezed past numerous hungry people waiting in line the way normal people do. *Not* my Boob Angel, though. She beckoned me in; there was no such thing as waiting in line for her. While finding her way to a two-top table, she gave me a knowing smile. With her bright grin staring back at me, I just knew I was home again.

As we stepped out of the restaurant after a yummy breakfast, we saw her. Sitting alone, on a green plastic outdoor chair, with her legs folded, waiting for a table, was none other than Pup's estranged wife.

Boob Angel stopped to say *"Hello,"* just a bit too loudly.

Boob Angel and Wife were friends, but Boob Angel's real friendship was mostly with Pup. As social propriety called for, she introduced us. Wife gave me a painfully long look over. She must have remembered

251

me from church many years ago but mentioned nothing of it. Much to my wild imagination, her eyes stopped at my crotch. Wife knew nothing of me or my relationship with her husband, she didn't even know he had been dating. I think guilt took over my thought process. Wife then proceeded to small talk with Boob Angel. Boob Angel was feeling conflicted, knowing she had introduced me to Wife's husband. Boob knew too much, and, at this moment, wished she knew nothing.

I stood respectfully between Boob and Wife, hiding behind my hat and sunglasses. In shorts, my long legs go on forever. Did they go on to expose the fact that they had been wrapped around her husband of thirty-plus years? I was going to vomit. I had so much tummy-churning gas that I finally burped. I'd trade a burp for the hiccups any day. Batman undies were in place.

In that moment, I specifically remembered the fact that her husband, also known as Pup, had told me that he did not want anyone else in the "bat cave." Were we going steady if he wanted to claim ownership of the bat cave? How could I take a superhero reference and turn it into an exclusive relationship with my married boyfriend? I stood there with a whole superhero scenario running through my mind. Suddenly, I needed a cape and high heels, or go-fast get-me-out-of-here shoes, or a phone booth. I needed some escape route, please!

I couldn't do this; I could not be this girl. What superhero disappears in a flash? Or was that a magician?

Boob Angel was probably doing a dance on the inside, knowing I was dating Wife's husband. My mind was racing. I did not want to meet Wife like this, *no*. I didn't really want to ever meet her, except maybe at a family barbecue with her new boyfriend by her side. Lord, I was completely losing it. Why today, why now?

Yet, there we were, three women acting casual, two women knowing things the other one didn't . . . dread was rising in my stomach once again. Boob Angel proceeded to talk way too fast, clearly freaking out. She was chattering like a nervous chipmunk. In turn, my legs were trembling.

The worst part about it, if there could have been a worst part, was that the more Boob Angel rattled on, the more she revealed. Boob Angel mentioned that I was single and that I had a multitude of boyfriends. She even mentioned the Bentley in my garage. She disclosed the fact that the guy who owned said Bentley was an ex (Lover). How much more was she going to say? Standing silently felt like a slow painful death; this was a nightmare. I began getting anxious and wondered what would spill from Boob Angel's pretty, glossy lips next.

Incredulous, I wondered, "Oh my God, what is she rambling on about?"

Boob Angel couldn't stop herself. It was like watching a runaway train with no brakes on a rainy day in the mountains. Meanwhile, my not so innocent phone began vibrating away in my back pocket. Pup was emailing me as I was being held hostage by the rules of politeness. I emailed back and let him know, right off the bat, where I was, with whom, and who was standing in front of me, his *Wife*.

After what seemed like forever, I mean, the earth was spinning like a cosmic collision, time held no bearing. I told Boob Angel we had to get to Bub's boat, my temporary home at sea. Sweat was now dripping down the back of my legs as well as forming on my upper lip. This just made her chat faster, if that was possible. Now, she started to sound like she was speaking a foreign language. Was she even speaking English? All her dizzy words were lost to me. How could Wife keep up with her? I was impressed. I thought Wife looked at my crotch again and held a gaze there. It was like a Mexican standoff, but more like a crotch stare off?

Who would blink first? I was losing my mind—my vagina had not blinked in years.

"It was a pleasure to meet you," I said to Wife, painfully lying through my breakfast-filled teeth.

I had always had a heart for Wife, and this was no exception. I had been in her shoes. I had been lied to by my husband, and it was awful. Pup and I had had numerous conversations about Wife. Boob Angel and I both shared with Pup how sorry we felt toward Wife. It had been deplorable, knowing she had not seen the whole picture yet. Pup constantly lied to her about me. I hated being that girl, the one who was always lied about. I was *the lie*.

Walking away from this moment with Wife, I turned to Boob Angel and said, "I am going to hell. I am going to hell. I am going to hell!"

I repeated the statement several times, mirroring Boob Angel's crazy mouth that I had just witnessed.

Boob was still wired up from the encounter and retorted, "No, no, no you're not, no way. Hell . . ."

Then she awkwardly laughed, "They won't even let you in!"

We began nervously laughing in hysterics, not knowing where to take the fateful moment.

I think we needed a drink. Was it five o'clock yet? Who the hell cares.

Pup called and quickly joined us on Bub's boat, my home on the sea. He passed his wife by twenty yards on his right to get to us. Pup was concerned and loving toward Boob Angel and I. I saw him wanting to take care of us; his focus was on our hearts. Love and life can be so fragile, and I was feeling especially frail after that moment. How could I ever imagine a future with him and integrate into his family after today? No amount of fantasizing would allow me to see past that. Yet, on the other side, how could I not imagine a future with Pup? It was so confusing. With Pup, looking at the future was strictly off limits.

I could see why. I had just met her, Wife.

That's the reason we had broken up so many times, or rather tried to. The rationalizing attempts lead me back to heartache, so there was no logic in love. Love can be a battlefield of crazy choices, what my heart wants may not always be healthy. That's how I had been processing my thoughts and feelings about Pup. I was drawing closer to healthy choices. I did not want to consider a life without my Pup, but it was time to.

Pup To The Pound

"I'm not responsible enough to have puppies."
—Logan Marshall-Green

IT WAS TIME TO RECOGNIZE THE RELATIONSHIP THAT WOULD leave no happy ending for anyone. After meeting Pup's wife in the harbor, and, after our numerous failed attempts at breaking up, there was no resolution in sight. We had tried to manage, control, and make sense of a relationship gone wrong. It was simply time to end a love that seemed impossible to end. But, what was even more impossible was for us to continue.

Boob Angel had recently seen Pup and Wife on a dinner date. I was done. I knew I had to be real and raw. I could not fail at this break-up any longer.

It was unlike me to be mean. but mean was called for. Mustering up a strong bitch, I could do this. I felt sick, but I had felt sick over Pup so many times before. I had a hard time turning my heart away from this man. I was trapped in a love spell. I called him and we agreed to meet at his apartment. We had taken a break to see if that would help us disconnect. It had been a few weeks since we had seen one another. This time it had to be different. I was losing my best friend and naively wished we could remain friends, but I knew better.

Well crap, the time apart did not matter. Seeing his wife and all the evidence laid out before me did not matter either, we were still in love. I knew I still loved him, but this was toxic for me and fucked up for him, never mind his wife sitting alone at the harbor. How could I be with him after meeting her? What kind of horrible person had I become?

I walked into the familiar space, the scene of the crime of passion, the apartment. In every corner, we had loved. There was no space that naked us did not find. I was going soft in the head, and, once again, tried to reason a way to keep my Pup.

That is the thing about bad choices; they are like a drug. One last time always seems so reasonable. One last fix, I swear! I needed to attend a meeting of bad girls that make dumb choices; was I *that girl?* I was that girl! I had to walk away without the fix. I was obsessing over a man that was really never really mine. I could no longer be his lie, and we both knew it.

He held me in his arms, shaking like a leaf. Pup had bought flowers, a refrigerator filled with food, and five bottles of wine that sat on top of the kitchen counter. His idea of our meeting was looking much different than mine.

Although we had not started speaking, I could hear the words that were not being said. This human moment was louder than any sound I had ever heard. His silent noise differed greatly from mine; his wanted to hang on to us. My mind was screaming: *wife, wife, wife.*

Breaking the deafening silence, Pup said, "I missed you so much."

Feeling pissed and building steam, I snapped, "Is that so?"

Hearing myself, I took a deep breath and tried to sound less awful.

He poured us a glass of wine and went into his same speech, "We have shared such great moments."

I heard him, but I was done with moments. Too many moments and too much awareness of his other life was in front of me, it was too late. This dualism had to stop. How was it possible that a man could lead two lives? You hear about it, but it is always on the news and two states away, or someone else's mess.

Even the neighbors in Pup's complex knew we were together. I was part of his life at the apartment. It was *our* life that existed behind the guarded gates. It was a fleeting life, as he ran off to his family life and I stayed behind in a state of what? Waiting for coffee to be served up with a side of sex in the morning? I was picking up scraps. This apartment held too many memories. What had I reduced myself to? I hated this me, I understood this me, I gave grace to this me. I needed to learn to forgive this me.

"You need to date your wife, you need to have moments with her," I calmly said it and meant it.

"You need to love me enough to let me go. Do you love me?" I continued.

"Of course," Pup uttered, and he meant it.

"I love you . . ." His words just hung in the air.

"God, please help me, I love you," Pup said, like I didn't know. Like I didn't hear him the first time, like I didn't know it said, or unsaid. His hands went to his face and he covered his eyes. He did not want to see. Tears rolled down easily.

I slipped out of the dining room chair and crawled to his feet. I rested my head on his thigh and took a moment to just breathe. Then my pleading eyes looked up to him, filled with tears.

"This is not healthy for us, this kind of love is hurtful and confusing," I said.

He placed his hand on my shoulder and began to rub my back, trying to comfort me.

He said, "I am not ready to let you go . . . I will die without you."

"Then die . . . I will not be your lie any longer. I will not be anyone's lie."

Pup then said, with tears racing down his cheeks, "I know I am a married man."

It was an honest moment for him. With both hands, Pup again covered his face. He created a moment alone with himself, a moment hidden from me. Would it have been different if his beautiful hands I adored so much wore a wedding band? I would never know, he never did, so it had not factored in.

"I will not be able to fully love you until I have divorce papers in my hand."

Pup then held his hand up as if it had papers in it. A vision that would forever stay with me to strengthen my resolve. I knew that no matter what he said, I was done. The end of him quickly ran through me like a juice cleanse, one last time.

I deserved more, and, one day, my body would catch up to my words. I would be able to embrace a true love. I began feeling the effects of letting go of a big love that I so willingly let in.

One day, when the emotions settled and ambivalence set in, I knew I could finally be free. My mind would be able to drift for days without a single thought of this man that did so much for me. He had once been my King and my Devil, I was sadly aware he would someday become just a memory. I would be free. I learned more about myself and my choices during this part of my journey. I found my voice, a part of me that once hid in fear. It could now proudly claim it's truth. One day I would be able to take away the love and leave behind the married man. There were no papers in his beautiful ring-less hand. I would not circle like a vulture waiting for the unseemly remains of a marriage that was over. I was not that hungry. I was not that desperate. My sick stomach agreed. That was not meant to be.

Pup and I were in painful accord. Our affair was over. He was in no way ready to end his marriage, nor was he ready to be honest about us. If the truth sets you free, then this lie had laid us to rest.

At that moment, a part of me wanted to die; at that moment, a part of me had to die.

I lived and slowly became proud of myself for finally having the strength to walk away.

I managed to find grace for myself and for my Pup.

FINDING A NEW MAN

"All truths are easy to understand once they are discovered; the point is to discover them."
—GALILEO GALILEI

I HAD A FEELING AT THE BEGINNING OF SUMMER THAT MAN NUMber three would come into the picture. Scratch that, my half boyfriends were officially part of my tattered past. Being out of my home all summer begged for many possibilities. I was enduring deep frustration as a result of my current lack of love, coupled by day-to-day mending of my heart, followed by finding my new rhythm without a man. All the while I was disconnecting from my home of nearly three decades.

I was assuming my next man would be heterosexual, but that was closed-mindedness on my part. My New Man was loud, proud, gorgeous as hell, and vibrantly gay. I felt an instant connection with him and his dog. I met him at an outdoor cafe and wanted to tell him right there that we were meant to be the best of friends. Social parameters—and the obvious fear that he might rightly think of me as insane—kept me from doing so. Instead, I ended up babysitting his dog Agadore, and I fell in love with him too.

New Man moved to Dana Point, California from the East Coast. I met him while he was pulling himself out of a ten-year relationship, slowly mending and trying to find himself. He adopted a dog, Agadore, New Man then started to heal. He lived in the gated community of Niguel Shores in Dana Point. A step up from the boat I had grown so fond of. He had two bathrooms and two bedrooms! Yippee! Overnights at his home were always welcomed. Go figure, his coffee was the best! We shared pitchers of margaritas and solved the unsolvable mysteries concerning life, love, and moreover, *men*. Time with New Man had a sweet perspective. It was absolutely necessary throughout my journey of a man for every purpose.

If I, in fact, had a man for every purpose, then I really scored big with this one. On one glorious sun-filled afternoon, we walked a few blocks to the beach to watch the sunset. There were some lucky neighbors that had that same idea. I was wearing a long grey dress that was very much see-through. I didn't care, I was at the beach, and he was gay.

While sipping on wine coolers, New Man told me, "Don't wait for one of your guys to step up. Have your own space and independence."

Then he said, as if he'd already experienced such, "You don't want to be reliant on a man."

"Form your own independence, it is strong, it is sexy. Go with that girl . . ."

He continued, "Men chase after that, will always chase after that, that one sexy minx who is just out of reach. We can't help it, we are guys."

I began piecing together New Man's wise words. I loved it when men, or people in general, revealed their truths. New Man had possibly offered up some of the best advice of my life: be strong in who you are, be yourself. It was time to let the kickass girl in me rule like a soft-loving Queen! We all have our own truths, and during this sunset and margarita-filled moment, I was blessed to hear New Man's take on men.

This advice came from someone who knew men, who loved men, who dated men, and in fact, was a man.

"I better pay attention," I thought. I better pay very close attention.

If my mother ever doled out advice for me, which she did not, it would have sounded something like New Man's words. Maybe the magic of Agadore would have a healing effect on me as well.

I was in no way surprised that I had been placed in just the right spot, at just the right time. I was spending quality time with a wonderful guy who I found great laughter with. He was tender-hearted and smart.

We cried on each other's shoulders and laughed together. We both liked men and were questing to understand them, moreover, to understand ourselves. New Man suggested we become roommates. This was the best offer I had been presented with in a very long time. I took his suggestion into serious consideration.

Part Four

Back In Bed

"If you think you're too small to have an impact,
try going to bed with a mosquito."
—Anita Roddick

I LAY IN BED ALONE, IN MY FAVORITE PAIR OF COMFY BATMAN UN-
derwear. Egyptian cotton has never felt so welcoming. It is surrounding my skin and creating cotton happiness. I realized my truth. It has
never really been about the sheets or the men that I once called home.

My toes curl up only to feel the comfort of my own skin. And yes, I
will find a companion to call home again . . . but never again will I feel
as innocent as I did on my journey to find a surrogate home. It is vital
that I find peace within myself, comfort deep within my heart, especially on those nights when I toss in unrest as my own skin turns against me
in a moment of doubt.

I know there will be times where I may need to get new sheets to
remind my skin of its wonder inside the presence of something new
and crisp. For now, I am pushing toward being present, leaving behind
the past. I am finding out it was as much about my own journey as it
was about any one man. Getting to know that the very best person I
have, the one I go to sleep with and wake up with every day, is me. I am
learning of the peace that lives within my own slumber.

Finding The 'Me' In My 'Me'-N

"Tell me and I forget. Teach me and I remember.
Involve me and I learn."

—Benjamin Franklin

I HAD PUT MEN AND LOVERS AHEAD OF MYSELF FOR YEARS. My choices and decisions in life had always been based on whom I was dating, whom I was loving, or whom I was raising at the time. I morphed into the "us," losing a bit of myself along the way. I was always running. I was always looking to gain control, while running away from the voices that sent me into a whirlwind of anxiety and hiccups.

The voices from my childhood home sent me on top of my horse. With my siblings, I struggled to find my inner peace. While on top of my horse, the world turned peacefully silent.

Later in life, it was the men's voices that took over my life. I was listening to all of their opinions of me, while hopelessly chasing after acceptance, approval, and comfort. I was certain that was what I desperately needed at the time: validation.

My children's voices and needs also came before my own. Their needs took center stage for most of my adult life. It took me a very long time to find my own voice. To become aware of the fact that I was not only good and fine as an individual, but that my voice mattered.

It was time for me to make a clear shift. It was time to put myself first for once. I had lived for my children. I had lived for my men, but when had I lived for myself? I needed to live for myself now.

I am happy, and it is okay to be single. I am grateful for the relationships around me today. Yes, all the men, and all the girlfriends as well. I am grateful that I was getting a better glance at myself through all of these relationships.

My daughter, the wise one, told me once, "The only thing we can take with us are the relationships we build. The love that is reflected in those relationships."

I am grateful for all the past relationships that I have known. Each person has become a part of the tapestry woven into my patch-worked soul.

Mantras:

"I am blessed in the relationships around me."

"I am blessed in the relationship I have with myself."

A Man For Every Purpose

"I am not trying to give an image of a fairytale,
perfect, everything else, I am just being myself."
—Rebecca Loos

Having a "Man For Every Purpose" has been illuminating. I think, in some ways, I have always had a man for every
purpose. Actually, sorting it out and reflecting on my role in these relationships has done wonders. I trust love is out there for me to find that
one special man. If there is ever a moment of uncertainty, it is only a
temporary mindset. Love is all around me, all the time, and every day.

I have learned many lessons on this heartbreaking, heart-awaken-
ing journey. There is no compromise when it comes to falling in love.
Love wholeheartedly and unashamedly! Life is as big as we make it, and
we are offered love daily. I must open my heart and recognize love when
it shows up. Will love round the corner like it did with Six? Only time
will tell. I'm leaning toward yes, of course.

I am perfectly alright with being single. Being single is not a disease
I have to be cured from, nor will I ever be cast off onto Lonely Island,
isolated from all couples. At this time, I will continue to adore my sexy,
saucy self and my many male friends. I will do this all while learning
every day a wee bit more about myself and the mystery of "man."
The moments throughout A Man for Every Purpose have proven to

271

be enormous failures as well as tremendous successes. Relationships all serve a unique purpose. It was always about me and what I attracted at that point in my journey.

It was *always* about the relationship I had with myself.

It really was *never* about them . . .

I understand that we are all made up of a team; I am not alone. As my daughter's words continue to echo in my head, "All anyone can take away from this world is the love they have left behind."

WHERE ARE THEY NOW?

"And in the end the love you take is equal to the love you make"

—THE BEATLES, *ABBEY ROAD*

Dream Mate: He is living happily ever after with his bride and their teenage son in Newport Rhode Island. I've heard rumors he has a male secretary.

Cub: He has been spotted at the local gym. I haven't seen him in over a decade.

Numeral Duce: Once our son turned eighteen, he sold his home and moved to Washington State, where he is from. We saw each other at our son's graduation from the Navy. We are both proud of our son and kind toward one another.

Wrong Guy: Thankfully, I've never seen, nor heard, from him.

Don and Dawn: Soulfully married, living the dream in Monarch Beach, California.

Harley Guy: I ran into him at a party, he avoided eye contact. I didn't even get a hello.

Oregon Guy: Just chatted with him. He's flying all over the country, making commercials. Living on the McKenzie river in Eugene, Oregon. I'm still waiting for my next commercial.

Star Dresser: He has a baby girl, and is working hard with a new TV pilot. Blissfully planted in Los Angeles.

Oklahoma: He has the hottest girlfriend within five hundred miles. They just bought a home and are living together with horses on the property. We still chat now and again.

Exception: Working in health-care, sports, and acting. He came back from South Africa with gold medals at the transplant Olympics.

Benefit Friend: He is up to the same type of woman-business he had always been, going from girl to girl.

Big: I recently chatted with him. It had that fake feeling of "let's do lunch." He is happily living alone in his big home. He still has his online profile up and running for the eighth year in a row.

Big's Son: He runs a media group and handles my website, photography, and videos. I am blessed to have him on my team.

Healer: Moved to Maui for two years with her husband and two dogs, doing readings, healing, and spreading light all around her. She has moved back to San Clemente. That puts us dancing reggae on Sundays, yippee.

The Psychic: I reunited with her for lunch in Venice Beach, California. She graduated with her degree in Psychology. She is working in Los Angeles with trauma victims. We've connected as friends, lucky me!

Pooh: She is living the dream with her Luvie in Eugene, Oregon, with their two cats and two dogs, in their farm house on the McKenzie River.

My Daughter and her husband: They are happy as clams living in Santa Barbara with their female rescued German Shepherd, appropriately named Frankie Sinatra, changing the world with loving, heroic efforts. One kickass couple.

My parents: Loving one another in Orange County, California.

Six: I recently went to his sixtieth birthday party. So much family and love. I'm lucky to be friends with this passionate man and his loving family.

Favorite Mother-in-law: Living happily with her husband in San Clemente, California. She recently called to check on me.

Rebound Nice Guy: I happily ran into him in Santa Barbara. He became retired and sadly broke up with his girlfriend. I was able to apologize after many years about the way I broke up with him. We had closure.

Beebe: He has retreated into his man cave. I miss him and love him in a very big way.

Player: Same deal, different girl. I run into him upon occasion.

Dirty Little Secret: I hope that he has all that he desires. He tells me that there is nothing dirty in his sexual appetite; it is simply his preference.

The Piano Man: Living the dream. Singing nights at The Montage. His beautiful wife is selling homes in Orange County, and the lovely little Miss is growing up. A beautiful little human I treasure.

Lover: I never drove the Bentley to Tiburon. After three years in Oregon, he moved back to Rancho Santa Fe with his many pups. He has created an animal rescue foundation. So blessed we are friends; he seems to show up around every corner, even thousands of miles apart.

East Coast: He is living the dream in Corona Del Mar. We danced at a reggae Sunday, glad that we became friends after all.

Boob Angel: A million talents wrapped up into one spitfire-babe; I'm blessed to know her. I marvel at this gal and continue to take notes. She bought a historic church, Chapman Chapel of Orange, as a wedding venue, one more plate a'spinning. She's forever given up on setting me up.

Bub: Friends for life, he and sweet Lisa are living together with a small pup. Busy with travel, love, and fifteen shared grandchildren.

New Man: We both would like to find the "perfect man." Knowing there is no such thing, we are enjoying the "men" that we know. He and Agadore are thriving. Sadly, our roommate scenario never came to fruition.

Pup: He is still married, he held onto his apartment for three years. He recently gave it up and moved back home with his wife. He is one of the biggest-hearted humans I had ever known.

R2: I am fairly certain that he is blissfully planted in bachelorhood, rooted deep in comfort. No single girl can encroach on that, nor should she.

Me: Oh, and, as for me? I have leased my home, leaving behind much in order to create more. I am finding freedom in the unknown and an ability to adapt. Honestly, it's sometimes frustrating, with dark moments, giving up my familiar has altered my being. This is where the growth is for me; becoming aware that this is my adventure. I have to be at home with myself, ugh. I have landed in a town that I have been in love with for decades, Santa Barbara, doing a job I could not have ever dreamt of! I am riding horses. Oh, and I met a man, one very special guy. (*Dreams really can come true . . . .Let's hope!*)

And Thank You

"The first responsibility of a leader is to define reality. The last is to say thank you. In between, the leader is a servant."

—Max de Pree

Thank Yous come in the beginning. This may be more fun as you might try attempting to put a name to a character. After all, we are just six degrees of separation.

For the many men that have been in my life starting with my childhood, knowingly or unknowingly, guiding me along the way, a heartfelt thank you. Be it good or be it bad, it was all a part of my journey. For those I may have forgotten, or did not acknowledge, sorry. It was just a story after all…From my heart to yours:

Scott, Chris, Terry, Bill, Paul, Saul, David, Dennis, Don, Mark, Bruce, Jeff, Ted, Brian, Mark, Charlie, Mike, Michael, Mike, Jon, Ricky, Joe, Gregg, Kyle, Sam, Roger, Howard, Jessie, Dave, Bennett, Kevin, Todd, Evan, Matt, Rick, Jim, Hezy . . . Hugs.

"Isn't it amazing what clever girls can do?"

—J.M. Barrie, *Peter Pan*

Katie L. Lindley

My girls, my homies, my female clan, that listened and loved me through my obsessive tears, droning on, and on, and over, and over, about men: From my heart to yours, Namaste:

> Vanessa Wood, Leslie Jodoin, Becky Randall, Abagail Starr, Cheryl Gayle, Ronda Mulligan, Dana Christakes, Lori Shelton, Avonelle Lindley, Annelle Morton, Donna McCoy, Launa Hall, Rosie Sandoval, Carolyn Innes, Melinda Herrick, Delores Sirott, Cindi Cooper, Barbara Spears, Leilani Baker, Deb Vejar, Heather Heinz, Terry Stanley, Michelle Obirny, Donnie Fergit, Rebecca Atwater, Laura Fitzpatrick, and Anna Sherry. My girlfriends are all strong vibrant confident women.

Unending gratitude to Karen Dominique Dickinson, who sat with me, wine in hand, for hours poring over this story, laughing along the way of our journey of giggles. In more settings, and in more men's homes than we care to count, but surely laugh about. "What the hell is the Wi-Fi password?" Cheers to forever trying "Ilovekatie" and it never working. The day that password works may be the day I have found the "one" man for most *all* purposes, thank God. One of us had to know how to write, and it was her.

A House For Every Purpose
My Journey from Pillow to Pillow

Based On A True Story . . . Mostly

> "I once had a rose named after me and I was
> very flattered. But I was not pleased to read the
> description in the catalogue: no good in a bed,
> but fine up against a wall."
>
> —Eleanor Roosevelt

WAKING UP IN THE MIDDLE OF THE NIGHT, WONDERING WHAT
pillow my head was resting on. Another house, another pillow.
My eyes remained closed, and I reached back to touch the headboard.
That should tell me where I am. A marker to remain safe. In the forest,
ribbons are tied to trees so one can be rescued.

Now I am fumbling my way with my fingers, trying to get my bearings as to where I was sleeping. This was a bizarre way of understanding where I was. I listen for clues to place myself. Do I hear seals, a fog horn, a train? I am in such a deep sleep I am not sure if I am alone or not, moreover, who I might be sharing the sheets with.

As hapless as that sounds, I was fairly well organized and getting used to my newfound nomadic life. My overnight pink bag was always nearby, so I did have some constant in my inconsistent days.

Karen Dominique Dickinson
Contributing Author

Karen Dominique Dickinson has been writing her entire life. Instead of running around with dolls while growing up, she ran around with pens and paper. Karen stepped into "A Man For Every Purpose" after reading one page and falling completely in love. She then sat down with Katie L. Lindley and took her beautifully written ideas and helped mold them into a poetic masterpiece. As Katie's writing coach, Karen learned a lot about the author as well as herself. The journey became one of self-discovery for both the author and the coach. "We spent hours with wine glasses in our hands and laughter in our hearts trying to come up with words that could someday be read by the world," Karen said. You may contact Karen for coaching or writing services by visiting KarenDominique.com.

ABOUT THE AUTHOR

Katie L Lindley is the founder of sexlovemantra.com, where she blogs often and candidly about her personal quest for true romance in 21st century America. Her first book is a work of heart. It chronicles her adventures, her insights, the misses . . . and hits! Katie is currently living in Santa Barbara, California where she is working on the next book in the series: *A House for Every Purpose: My Journey from Pillow to Pillow.*

Is true love a fairy tale that can't even make it through one night? Or is it something attainable that will last?

In *A Man for Every Purpose*, we explore the story of one woman's very personal and refreshingly honest exploration of relationships (the good, the bad, and the strange) and all that comes with searching for the "right" one.

For years, Katie thinks she has it made—happy in a steady marriage—but life is nothing if not unpredictable. As her first true love vanishes before her eyes, she is forced to understand the world of love, sex, and relationships. Is one better than the other? Can all three things exist simultaneously, or is a woman doomed to settle for less than what her heart, mind, and body desires?

In her search for Mr. Right, our endearing and fearless heroine dis-

Katie L. Lindley

covers a bit more than she bargained for. Not only about the men who occupy different roles in her life, but about the person she's set out to be as well.

A Man for Every Purpose is cheeky, smart, entertaining, and ultimately, wise. It will make you laugh and cry as you read about her endless attempts searching for what she thinks is true love. Along the way, you may see yourself in our heroine, or, even some of her men. And we guarantee you'll identify with the realities of love and dating in modern America.

> "The course of true love never did run smooth."
> —WILLIAM SHAKESPEARE

A Man For Every Purpose has a Facebook page, visit us at www.facebook.com./KatieLLindley

www.KatieLLindley.com
www.Sexlovemantra.com
www.amanforeverypurpose.com
Instagram: Sexlovemantra

Look forward to book 2 . . .

A House For Every Purpose—My Journey From Pillow to Pillow . . .

Where leaving my home of twenty-nine years, I discovered more than a soft place to fall . . . The journey continues onto moments I couldn't even predict!

Do I finally settle down and find that one special man?
Do I finally settle down and find that one special town and home?
Does a man from my past reenter with new possibilities?
Does my heart's desire become fulfilled?
Or do my expectations shift?

Join the fun, quotes, blogs, photos, and new adventures at sexlovemantra.com

Cheers!
From my heart to yours, with much love, Katie

References

Karen Dominque Dickinson, who patiently guided me. I had the story: she coached me and shaped many words through endless hours to become a book.

Karendominique.com

Many thanks to Katie McCoach who edited with passion and perceptive understanding, gently pulling me along forming the book! Much gratitude for her beautiful insight.

Katiemccoach.com

Evan Dorian, who helped me to "brand" myself, built my website, and shot all the photos/videos, a talented visionary.

Melinda De Ross, who designed the book cover.

Cheri Lasota, who designed the ebook and print book.

CheriLasota.com/Authors-Assembler

Healer: Hearttosoulawakening.com
Evan Dorian: Dorianmediagroup.com
Boob Angel: ChapelofOrange.com
Oregon Guy: Cappellimiles.com
Lover: Animal rescue; Rescueexpress.org
Myself: Sexlovemantra.com

Alison Enriquez, of Ali E. Photography, who made sure Karen Dominique Dickinson got the perfect shot. Aliephotography.com.